Quick and Easy
ELECTRIC PRESSURE COOKER COOKBOOK

Quick and Easy
ELECTRIC PRESSURE COOKER COOKBOOK

BARBARA SCHIEVING

FAST AND
FOOLPROOF
RECIPES FOR
EVERY KIND OF
MACHINE

NEW SHOE PRESS

Brimming with creative inspiration, how-to projects, and useful information to enrich your everyday life, quarto.com is a favorite destination for those pursuing their interests and passions.

First Published in 2023 by New Shoe Press, an imprint of The Quarto Group,
100 Cummings Center, Suite 265-D, Beverly, MA 01915, USA.
T (978) 282-9590 F (978) 283-2742 Quarto.com

New Shoe Press titles are also available at discount for retail, wholesale, promotional, and bulk purchase. For details, contact the Special Sales Manager by email at specialsales@quarto.com or by mail at The Quarto Group, Attn: Special Sales Manager, 100 Cummings Center, Suite 265-D, Beverly, MA 01915, USA.

ISBN: 978-0-7603-8348-3
eISBN: 978-0-7603-8349-0

The content in this book was previously published in *The Electric Pressure Cooker Cookbook* (Harvard Common Press 2017) by Barbara Schieving.

Library of Congress Cataloging-in-Publication Data available

Photography: Barbara Schieving.

*To my husband and my kids—the joy in my life
and the reason I pressure cook.*

And to my Pressure Cooking Today *blog readers—
those who have been there from
the beginning and those just joining me on this
pressure cooking journey.*

Contents

Introduction

Getting the Most from Your Electric Pressure Cooker

There is a pressure cooking renaissance going on right now. You can make better tasting meals in a fraction of the time using today's modern, easy-to-use electric pressure cookers. As with any new tool, there are a few things you'll need to know before you get cooking—let's get started.

Advantages of Using an Electric Pressure Cooker

Pressure cooking, in general, offers certain advantages over the oven, stove, or slow cooker.

- **Faster cook time.** Electric pressure cookers let you cook meats, stews, soups, beans, stocks, and broths in a fraction of the time they take to cook on the stove, in the oven, or with the slow cooker—and foods still taste like they've been cooking for hours!

- **Better flavor.** The pressure inside the pot raises the boiling point, which forces liquid into tough foods, making them tender, and the high heat promotes caramelization, adding depth of flavor.

- **Better nutrient retention.** The longer you cook fruits and vegetables in water, the more nutrients they lose. When you pressure cook your vegetables, you use a shorter cook time—keeping nutrients in your food and making your meals healthier.

- **Cook from frozen.** Forget to thaw the meat? No problem! No thawing required before pressure cooking. (This works best for smaller cuts of meat.)

- **Cost savings.** Ovens and stoves use a lot of energy as they cook. Pressure cookers require less energy, have shorter cook times, and don't heat up your house.

- **Easy cleanup.** One-pot cooking means only one pot to clean.

In addition, there are some unique advantages to electric pressure cookers instead of stovetop pressure cookers:

- **Safety.** Electric pressure cookers have several built-in safety features to prevent mishaps, including automatic pressure control, heating and pressure sensors, lid detection, and heating plates that distribute heat evenly.

- **Convenience.** You don't have to stand at the stove to adjust the heat so that whatever you're cooking doesn't boil over—the electric pressure cooker automatically regulates the heat and pressure. Go play with your kids, pay bills, or clean the kitchen and set the table while the electric pressure cooker does all the work.

- **Consistent results.** Once you figure out the right cook time for your pressure cooker you'll come back to a perfectly cooked dish—every time.

- **Keep Warm setting.** Unlike a stovetop pressure cooker, you don't need to worry about being home to turn off the pot; most electric pressure cookers automatically switch to the Keep Warm setting when the pressure cook time ends.

Getting to Know Your Electric Pressure Cooker

The earliest pressure cookers were created on a simple concept: Food cooks hotter and faster inside a pressure-sealed pot. (The scientific explanation involves raising the boiling point of water, which allows pressure cookers to cook food about 40°F (4.5°C) hotter than it could cook on the stovetop.) Electric pressure cookers use technology to enhance this process—for instance, by using sensors to regulate the temperature and pressure automatically inside the pot during cooking.

Electric pressure cookers place the cooking pot inside a housing unit that includes a heating element and sensors as well as the operating controls. The lid contains a gasket to ensure it fits snugly against the housing and a pressure release valve and small float valve that allow pressure to release safely, if needed.

There are many brands of electric pressure cookers currently on the market. (Some brands prefer the term "multi-cookers" because they offer slow cooking features; however, they all operate similarly, and, for simplicity, I refer to them all as pressure cookers throughout the book.) I own several brands and often use two at the same time, including:

Instant Pot. The Instant Pot pressure cooker is the one I use most in my kitchen. I really like the stainless steel pot for browning and that the cooker tells me when it's preheated and ready to sauté ingredients. It's quiet, comes in a variety of models, and sizes range from 3 quart to 8 quart (2.8 to 7.5 L). The Instant Pot is a multi-cooker, and some models offer high- and low-pressure settings and also function as slow cookers, rice cookers, and yogurt makers.

Fagor. Fagor has been selling stovetop pressure cookers worldwide for decades, and they've recently entered the electric pressure cooker market with two quality products: the LUX multi-cooker and the more affordable Premium Pressure Cooker. The LUX was recently chosen as the top-rated multi-cooker in Good Housekeeping's "Multi-Settings Cooker Reviews." I really like the buttons on the Fagor pressure cookers. Fagor pressure cookers come with a nonstick pot, though they recently began offering the LUX LCD with a stainless steel pot.

Power Pressure Cooker. The Power Pressure Cooker is one of the best-selling electric pressure cookers on the market. It comes in three sizes—6 quart, 8 quart, and 10 quart (5.7, 7.5, and 9.5 L)—and it's an affordable option for a larger pressure cooker. Currently it offers only a nonstick pot, which makes for easy cleanup but doesn't brown quite as well as a stainless steel pot.

Cuisinart. My first electric pressure cooker was a 6-quart (5.7 L) Cuisinart, so I have a fondness for it. It doesn't tout itself as a multi-cooker, and I like the straightforward buttons. Select High or Low Pressure, set the cook time, and press start—no wondering whether to use the chicken button or the stew button. It comes with a nonstick pot that can get scratched if you're not careful.

As the popularity of electric pressure cookers has exploded, many manufacturers have added electric pressure cookers or multi-cookers to their offerings. Breville, Farberware, Black & Decker, and T-fal now offer 6-quart (5.7 L) electric pressure cookers, which operate similarly to the models I've discussed.

Electric Pressure Cooker Parts

The various electric pressure cooker brands use slightly different terms to refer to the cooker's parts; however, these parts are similar among all brands. For your convenience, I've included a quick explanation of the terms I use throughout the book.

Cooking pot. Made of stainless steel, ceramic, or nonstick aluminum, this removable pot is where the magic happens. (Do not confuse this with the housing, also called the exterior or stationary pot—you can seriously damage your electric pressure cooker if you try to cook without the cooking pot inside the housing.)

Pressure release valve. Also called a pressure limit valve, pressure regulator knob, steam release handle, steam release reset button, and rapid release button, this plastic piece is located on the lid's exterior and controls whether the pressure inside the pot is allowed to escape. While the different brands have different names for this knob, it's the same basic principal: Use it to either seal the pressure cooker or to allow the steam to escape and let the pressure release quickly.

Sealing ring. Made of tough, food-grade silicone, this removable ring attaches to the underside of the lid. When locked in place, this ring creates the airtight seal that lets the pressure cooker come to pressure. This is also called a silicone gasket, rubber grommet, or rubber gasket, depending on the brand.

Float valve. Also called a floating valve or pressure limit valve, this small valve is one of the safety features of electric pressure cookers. As your pressure cooker comes to pressure, the float valve is pushed up until the mini gasket seals the cooker. When the float valve rises, the lid locks to prevent it from being opened while the contents are at pressure. When this valve drops, you can carefully remove the lid and continue with your recipe.

Selecting a Button

As with the pressure cooker components, even though different pressure cooker brands use different names for the buttons, all pressure cookers operate similarly. The recipes in this cookbook are designed to work in any electric pressure cooker—regardless of what the control panel looks like or how many buttons it has.

If you have a multi-cooker with additional buttons, your user manual should have an in-depth explanation of the different buttons and how they work. I recommend familiarizing yourself with them. However, these manuals don't always clarify that the buttons are simply convenience settings with preprogrammed cook times. Pressure cookers currently on the market cannot sense what you are actually cooking in the pot.

So, don't worry—you're not going to "mess up" by using the Meat button when you cook chicken soup. Nearly all the buttons on electric pressure cookers cook at High Pressure, so it really doesn't matter if you choose the Meat, Stew, or Poultry button. You can even cook desserts using the Meat button with no problem, as long as you adjust the cook time accordingly.

Initial Walk-Through

An easy way to familiarize yourself with your electric pressure cooker is to test it using only water. The steps in this process are repeated every time you cook at pressure, though they won't always be written in this much detail in the recipe.

1. Place the pressure cooking pot inside the housing. Get in the habit of checking that the inner pot is there before you start pouring in ingredients!

2. Add 1 cup (235 ml) water to the pressure cooking pot.

3. Check that the lid is properly assembled with the sealing ring in position and the float valve in place. Close and lock the lid. Verify that your pressure cooker is positioned so that steam vents away from cabinets.

4. Make sure the pressure release valve is in the Sealed position. The term for this position varies by brand (Sealing for Instant Pot; Pressure for Fagor and Cuisinart). Read your user manual for the exact term on your electric pressure cooker.

5. Select the Manual/High Pressure setting and set 5 minutes for the cook time. (Or, to test a multi-cooker setting, select one of the preprogrammed pressure cooking buttons and set a 5-minute cook time.)

6. Watch while the pressure cooker does all the work. It takes about 5 minutes for the water to heat up and build pressure; some steam will release from the float valve while pressure is building. The steam causes the float valve to rise and seal, but the timer won't start until the pot reaches pressure—only then does the timer start counting down.

7. When the cook time ends, carefully turn the pressure release valve to the Venting position so that steam can escape and the pressure can release. Again, the exact term varies by brand (Venting for Instant Pot, Steam for Fagor). Avoid placing your hands, face, or arms directly over the valve—the steam is very hot and can burn. (When my daughter first started using her electric pressure cooker, the steam and the noise made her a little nervous, so she used a wooden spoon to turn the valve.)

8. Once the steam disperses completely, you should hear the float valve drop. When this happens, the lid unlocks. Carefully remove the lid, tilting it so that steam vents away from you. The pressure cooking pot is hot—use hot pads or silicone mitts to remove it.

9. Don't forget to turn off the pressure cooker! (Sometimes I unplug my pressure cooker to make sure it isn't still cooking on the Keep Warm setting without my noticing.)

That's it! Now that you're familiar with your pressure cooker, let's get started with some easy pressure cooking recipes, such as Cilantro-Lime Rice (page 255) or Strawberry Applesauce (page 274). Before you know it, you'll be making fabulous pressure cooker meals and wondering how you ever cooked without it!

Pressure Cooking Terminology

When my daughter first began using a pressure cooker, she was a little intimidated by the unfamiliar terms she encountered in my recipes. Many cooks who are new to pressure cooking feel this way; however, once you learn the terminology, you'll be confident and ready to get cooking.

Releasing Pressure

One of the first things to learn about pressure cooking is when and how to release the pressure. When the cook time ends, the cooker beeps. At this point, the recipe directs you how to release the pressure in the pressure cooking pot, using one of the following methods:

Natural pressure release. A natural pressure release is when you leave the pressure release valve in the Sealed position when the cook time ends; this lets the pressure release slowly, without you doing anything. After the cook time expires, most electric pressure cookers automatically switch to the Keep Warm setting and the pressure inside the cooking pot begins to drop slowly. Food inside the cooking pot continues to cook as the pressure decreases. A natural pressure release can take from 5 to 30 minutes—the time varies depending on the ingredients and amount of liquid in the cooking pot.

The pressure cooker will not open until all pressure is released. When the pressure is fully released, the float valve drops and the lid unlocks and opens easily. There is no beep or signal when the pressure is released, though sometimes you can hear the float valve drop if you're close by.

Use a natural pressure release any time you need to release the pressure gradually— particularly for soups and grains, which are known to foam inside the pressure cooking pot, and for large cuts of meat, which need to rest after cooking to tenderize the meat.

Quick pressure release. A quick pressure release (or rapid release) is when you turn the pressure release valve to the Venting position and let the steam release quickly after the cook time ends. (Remember,

the exact term for the valve varies by brand.) Unlike a natural pressure release, a quick pressure release results in a strong jet of steam coming from the pressure release valve. This is normal. If drops of liquid or foam start to emerge from the pressure release valve, simply switch the valve back to the Sealed position and use an intermittent pressure release (see following).

When you use a quick pressure release, you know the pressure is fully released when the steam fully dissipates and the float valve drops. You cannot unlock the lid until all the pressure is released.

A quick pressure release stops the cooking quickly to avoid overcooking; it is well suited for ingredients such as potatoes and vegetables that need to stop cooking while they're tender but still hold their shape.

Intermittent pressure release. An intermittent pressure release is the best way to release pressure for foods such as pastas, soups, and certain grains, which are prone to foaming or spitting if you try to release pressure with a quick release. With this method, you open and close the pressure release valve in intervals. This allows the pressure to escape more quickly than a natural pressure release and also prevents foam from coming out of the pressure release valve. With some foods, one or two closed intervals is all I need before I can leave the valve in the Venting position; with other foods, if the foaming is particularly bad, I will close the valve and wait a minute or two, then slide the valve to Venting again and continue opening and closing the valve as needed.

Abbreviated natural release. The different types of pressure releases can also be combined; for example, in many recipes in this cookbook, I let the pressure release naturally for a number of minutes, then use a quick pressure release to release any remaining pressure. Combining the two release options reduces waiting time yet gives you many of the benefits of a natural pressure release, such as reducing foam and tenderizing meats.

Keep Warm setting. When the pressure cook time ends, most models will automatically switch to the Keep Warm setting. This setting continues to heat food at a low temperature. Check your manual for details on how the Keep Warm setting works in your brand.

> ### TIP
>
> I prefer to turn off the pressure cooker after pressure cooking and set a kitchen timer to beep and remind me when to release the pressure. If you prefer to leave the pressure cooker on once the pressure cook time ends and let the Keep Warm setting keep track of the elapsed time, that's a great option too. The pressure begins to release naturally either way, so choose what works best for you.

Sautéing, Simmering, and Browning

Sautéing ingredients before cooking results in richer, more complex flavors; it is a cornerstone of cooking meats and soups and is necessary for flavorful gravies and sauces.

Since there is so much variety between machines, the recipes in this book use two terms for cooking techniques: Simmer/Sauté and Browning/Sauté. Use what works best according to your cooking preferences and your machine's capabilities. As you would sauté on a stovetop, use these buttons only when the lid is off.

Simmer/Sauté. When you see this term in a recipe, select either the Simmer or Sauté button. The Simmer feature uses a lower heat than the Sauté feature and is best for thickening sauces and soups.

Browning/Sauté. Likewise, when you see this term, use either the Browning or Sauté button to cook. The Browning feature uses a higher heat than the Sauté feature, so your meats and vegetables (such as onions, carrots, and celery) cook more quickly on Browning than on Sauté.

- Here are some tips to get the best results from the Browning/Sauté settings:
- Select the Browning/Sauté button to preheat the pot. Do not add any oil or ingredients to the cooking pot before it has finished preheating.

- Don't crowd the pot by adding too much food at the same time. This is especially important with meats—if they are packed tightly in the pot, they will steam, not brown.

- When cooking vegetables, stir frequently to promote even cooking. In contrast, when cooking meats, place the meat in the pot and do not stir. Periodically test with a fork by gently lifting part of the meat; do not turn it until the meat releases easily from the pot.

- If foods cook too quickly (for example, a sauce boiling too rapidly), use a hot pad to lift the inner pot a few inches (about 7.5 cm) away from the heating element on the bottom of the pot or remove the pot from the pressure cooker briefly. If your machine has the capability, switch to a lower heat setting.

- After you finish browning, many recipes have you deglaze, or add liquids to, the hot pan. When you brown vegetables or meats, they release juices that caramelize on the bottom of the pot, called fond, which adds delicious flavor to sauces and gravies. Adding a liquid—such as broth, juice, wine, or even plain water (don't use dairy, which could curdle)—loosens the fond from the bottom of the pot. Immediately after adding the liquid, stir, scraping up any browned bits from the bottom of the pot to flavor the sauce. The fond should be golden-brown to dark brown; if it turns black, your food will taste burnt.

Pressure Cooking Pointers

Read the entire recipe before cooking.
Few things in the kitchen are more frustrating than getting halfway through a recipe and realizing you don't have an ingredient or that the food needs to chill for hours before you can continue. Plus, having foods measured and chopped before you start cooking can help cut your stress level as you cook. In addition, many recipes have serving suggestions at the end, so reading to the end helps you plan ahead so that you have these items ready when you need them.

Understand recipe timing. While pressure cooking is fast, it doesn't happen in an instant. When you start the pressure cooker, the heating element turns on and starts to heat your food, building the steam that puts the "pressure" in pressure cooking. The time spent coming to pressure is similar to time spent preheating an oven or waiting for water to boil—it isn't counted in the cook time. The recipe cook time does not start until the pressure cooker reaches pressure. The time it takes for your pressure cooker to reach pressure could be as quick as 5 minutes when cooking with small amounts of liquid or as long as 30 minutes if your ingredients are cold or your pot is filled with lots of liquid.

Trust your senses. You'll be more successful and avoid mistakes in the kitchen if you learn to trust your instincts and your senses. Remove the cooking pot from the pressure cooker housing immediately if you smell burning while sautéing. Use a quick pressure release and open the lid if you see steam escaping from around the sides of the lid—you don't have a proper seal. Don't be afraid to take action if something doesn't seem right!

Recognize there's more than one right way to pressure cook. One of the best features of pressure cooking is its flexibility; often, there are many ways to approach cooking certain items. For example, I prefer to cook beans using a quick soak method (1 minute at pressure with 1 hour soak time), but you can also soak your beans overnight or even increase the pressure cook time in the recipe to accommodate the unsoaked beans. While none of these methods is "right" or "wrong," you will find you prefer some methods over others. Use what works best for you!

Use these recipes with a stovetop pressure cooker. All recipes in this cookbook can also be cooked in a stovetop pressure cooker. Simply bring your stovetop pressure cooker to pressure using a medium-high heat and then reduce the heat to the lowest setting necessary to maintain pressure. Start timing the cook time once your stovetop pressure cooker reaches pressure.

Use the minimum liquid required. The minimum amount of liquid required varies among the different brands of pressure cookers; consult your user manual to find your brand's minimum amount. However, many brands do not acknowledge that the minimum amount of liquid required can also depend on what you're cooking. Many ingredients release liquid as they cook, so you can use less liquid to begin with; for example, many of my chicken recipes use less than the minimum amount of water because the chicken releases liquid as it cooks.

Reduce or double recipes. When reducing a recipe, do not reduce the liquids below ½ to 1 cup (120 to 235 ml) cooking liquid.

You can generally use the same cook time specified in the original recipe, as the timing is based more on the thickness of the food than on the amount. Therefore, when you reduce a recipe, don't cut the cook time if the thickness of the food remains the same—especially when cooking meat. For example, whether you cook 2 pork chops or 6 pork chops, the cook time stays the same if all the pork chops are the same thickness.

When doubling a recipe, never fill the pot above the maximum fill line, typically two-thirds full or half full for foods that foam. (For this reason, I don't recommend doubling most pasta recipes in this book.) However, the same principles for cook time apply to doubling a recipe—as long as the thickness of the food is the same, you can generally use the recipe's original cook time. Be aware that a fuller pot takes longer to come to and release pressure, which increases the overall time, and you may need to reduce the recipe cook time to compensate.

High-altitude cooking. I live about 4,000 feet (1.2 km) above sea level, which is considered high altitude, and I occasionally need to change a recipe to adjust for that. Water boils at a lower temperature at high altitudes, so foods may need a slightly longer cook time. The technical rule is to add 5 percent more cook time at 3,000 feet (0.9 km) above sea level, 10 percent for 4,000 feet (1.2 km) above sea level, and so on, increasing by 5 percent every additional 1,000 feet (0.3 km). For example, at my altitude, if a recipe has a cook time of 30 minutes at sea level, technically I should add an extra 3 minutes to account for my altitude (0.10 × 30 minutes = 3 minutes extra).

That said, I rarely adjust for altitude, especially for foods with short cook times. Occasionally, I need to increase my cook times by a few minutes, especially with beans and grains. The recipes in this cookbook were tested at various altitudes and should not need any adjustment below 5,000 feet (1.5 km).

Check the temperature. As discussed in the Selecting a Button section (see page 14), your pressure cooker does not have a sensor that monitors what's cooking in the pot; each button only starts a preprogrammed cook time. The only way to know that your foods have reached the desired internal temperature is to use an instant-read thermometer.

I highly recommend getting in the habit of checking the temperature of pressure cooked foods. Common safe internal temperatures are as follows:

Breads and cakes	210°F	(100°C)
Baked potatoes	205°F	(96°C)
Chicken thighs and wings	180°F	(82°C)
Beef (well-done)	165°F	(74°C)
Chicken breasts	165°F	(74°C)
Turkey breasts	165°F	(74°C)
Ground beef (e.g., meatloaf)	155°F	(68°C)
Cheesecake	150°F	(65.5°C)
Beef (medium)	145°F	(63°C)
Fish	145°F	(63°C)
Pork	145°F	(63°C)
Beef (rare)	125°F	(51.5°C)

Thicken sauces and gravies after pressure cooking. Since pressure cooking requires liquid to achieve pressure, you'll generally thicken the flavorful pressure cooking liquids after pressure cooking. Using flour or cornstarch before pressure cooking can interfere with the pressure cooking process. Skip flouring your meat before browning it and use the flour in a slurry at the end to thicken the gravy.

I intentionally use many methods for thickening sauces and gravies in my recipes. A cornstarch slurry (whisking cornstarch and cold water) is probably the easiest method, but I also use a flour slurry, a roux, and blended vegetables, or I simmer sauces until they're reduced. As long as you add it after pressure cooking, there's no right or wrong thickener—switch them up as desired!

Cooking foods that foam or froth. Pressure cooking manuals often have warnings about cooking foods that foam in your pressure cooker, and for good reason—if cooked improperly, these foods can interfere with maintaining and releasing pressure. Common foods that froth and foam include pastas, soups, applesauce, beans and split peas, grains such as barley and oatmeal, and high-starch items like potatoes.

When cooking these foods, never fill the pot more than halfway. When the cook time ends, turn off the pressure cooker. Use a natural pressure release or an intermittent release, if necessary. If foam starts to come out of the pressure release valve, close it and wait a few minutes. If it works with your recipe, you may also add 1 or 2 tablespoons (15 to 30 ml) oil to the liquids in the cooking pot to reduce the foaming.

Cooking frozen meats. You get better results if you don't cook large cuts of frozen meat. A frozen roast doesn't brown well, cook as evenly, or absorb marinades—and it's hard to judge how much time it will take. However, if you want to cook from frozen, lots of people do. A good rule is to add 5 minutes of cook time per inch (2.5 cm) of thickness.

If your recipe calls for diced meat, but you forgot to defrost it the night before, use your pressure cooker to defrost and partially cook smaller cuts of frozen meats, such as chicken breasts. Simply pour 1 cup (235 ml) water into your pressure cooking pot, place a trivet in the bottom, and arrange the frozen chicken breasts on the trivet. Lock the lid in place. Select High Pressure and 1 minute cook time. When the cook time ends, turn off the pressure cooker. Use a quick pressure release. Remove the chicken from the pot and dice it into small pieces and continue with the recipe as directed.

Plan ahead. Making a meal plan that covers several days can save you even more time in the kitchen. Here are some tricks I use in my own cooking:

- When you bring meat home from the grocery store that you don't plan to use right away, cut it into bite-size pieces and freeze them flat. Bite-size pieces of meat thaw quickly, and you can use them frozen, without thawing or changing the recipe timing.

- Chop all the vegetables you'll use throughout the week at the same time so that they're ready to go on busy nights. Try to plan multiple meals that use the same vegetables, for instance, Creamy Chicken and Wild Rice Soup (page 56) and Quick-Cooking Chicken and Pierogi Dumplings (page 88). Store the different amounts in separate containers.

- Chopped onion freezes well, so if a recipe uses only half an onion, dice the entire onion and freeze half for another recipe.

- Freeze leftovers in single-serve portions. Many soups freeze well, but soups with noodles, potatoes, or rice freeze better if you freeze the noodles, potatoes, or rice in separate single-serving bags and reheat the two separately.

Troubleshooting Guide

Once in a while, something goes wrong in the pressure cooking process—it happens to even the best cooks! While many pressure cooker user manuals include brand-specific troubleshooting tips, here is a list of common problems I'm asked about by readers of my blog, Pressure Cooking Today, and my family and friends. In many cases, you can save the meal and get things back on track!

My lid won't lock into place. Sometimes if the liquid in the pot is hot, the steam pushes the float valve up and the safety mechanism won't let you lock the lid in place again. Make sure the pressure release valve is in the Venting position so that steam can release, and push the float valve down with the end of a wooden spoon.

Steam is coming from my lid. First, determine where the steam is coming from. If steam is coming from the pressure release valve, double-check that the valve is actually on the lid and is in the Sealing position. If steam is coming from the sides of the lid, it means the lid isn't sealing properly. There are a few reasons for this. To check, turn off the pressure cooker and use a quick pressure release. When the lid unlocks, remove the lid and check to see that the sealing ring and float valve are properly in place and free of any food particles. If either the float valve or sealing ring needs to be adjusted, wait until the lid is cool enough to handle to avoid the risk of burns.

In rare cases, steam escapes from the sides of the lid because the sealing ring is brittle or broken. If you notice issues with your sealing ring, unfortunately, the only solution is to replace it.

If you notice the steam early in the cooking process, adjust the pressure release valve or the lid and restart the High Pressure cook time. If you suspect a number of minutes went by before you noticed the problem, you may need to add more liquid to your pressure cooking pot or reduce the cook time—there's no hard rule for how much, so make your best guess.

It's taking forever for my ingredients to come to pressure. Remember, if you're cooking a dish like soup with a lot of liquid or if the ingredients are cold, it can take as many as 30 minutes for the pressure cooker to come to pressure.

If that's not the problem, you should double-check that the pressure cooker hasn't been unplugged by mistake. Also, check that you added enough liquid to the pressure cooking pot—pots cannot reach High Pressure without sufficient liquid, and bigger 8- and 10-quart (7.5 and 9.5 L) cookers may need more liquid than their smaller 5- and 6-quart (4.7 and 5.7 L) counterparts.

My meat scorches during the browning process. In these situations, there are a number of options. If possible, lower the heat setting and add more oil to the pot. If your recipe calls for them, be sure to have liquids measured and ready to add as soon as you're done browning. You can also lift the cooking pot away from the heating element to slow the cooking process briefly.

The cook time has ended, but my food isn't cooked. If your pasta or meat is nearly done, it's best not to return the pot to High Pressure. Rather, select Simmer/Sauté and finish cooking the dish on that setting. Food can also finish cooking on the Keep Warm setting—simply lock the lid in place and wait a few minutes more.

However, if your meat isn't close to the proper temperature or isn't as fall-apart tender as you'd like, lock the lid in place and pressure cook it again for additional time.

Also, if quicker-cooking foods such as vegetables are done, but your meat is not, remove these ingredients from the cooking pot and place them in a bowl covered with aluminum foil. Once your meat is cooked, return the vegetables to the cooking pot and heat through.

My sauce or gravy is too thin. Different ingredients release different amounts of liquid as they cook, so it's hard to judge the exact amount of thickeners you need before pressure cooking. For example, chicken injected with water before freezing releases more liquid than a fresh chicken breast. If your original recipe calls for a thickener, remember that thickeners need to reach a temperature near the boiling point before they activate (the exact temperature depends on your altitude), so continue to Simmer/Sauté to heat your dish. If your sauce is still is too thin, mix an equal ratio of thickener and water and add it to your sauce, or simply let the sauce simmer a little longer until the liquid reduces.

If the original recipe doesn't call for a thickener and your sauce is too thin, make a slurry by whisking 2 tablespoons cornstarch (16 g) with 2 tablespoons (30 ml) cold water until smooth and add it to your sauce.

My sauce or gravy is too thick. Don't be afraid to add a little extra liquid and stir until it reaches the consistency you like. The liquid doesn't have to be water—choose something that matches the ingredients in your meal.

My sauce or gravy is lumpy. Don't panic! Whisk the sauce vigorously, pour it through a fine-mesh sieve or strainer, or use an immersion blender to purée it smooth. Lumpy sauce often results from adding dry thickeners to a hot pot or from not stirring to incorporate them completely with the water, so double-check this step in the future.

My silicone ring smells like yesterday's dinner. Unfortunately, the silicone sealing ring and the mini gasket on the float valve have a tendency to take on strong smells, particularly after cooking flavorful, savory meats and soups. I've tried many remedies—lemon juice, vinegar, baking soda, and other food-safe cleaners—but haven't yet found anything that will completely get rid of the smell.

I like to use one ring for savory foods and an extra sealing ring only for mild foods, such as oatmeal and cheesecake. My daughter prefers to use three rings: one for savory dishes, one for breakfasts, and one saved just for cheesecake. She keeps her savory sealing ring inside a sealed zipper bag to keep the smell from transferring to her cupboards. In contrast, I like to store my lids upside down on the pressure cooking pot in my pantry so that the sealing ring has a chance to air out. Again, there's not a right or wrong way to do it.

CHAPTER 1

Breakfast

Breakfast is the most important meal of the day, and it's also my favorite meal. Here's a great selection of quick, get-you-out-the-door-fast recipes mixed with a handful of slow-morning indulgent recipes.

Very Berry Steel Cut Oats

My daughter and her family are crazy about pressure cooker steel cut oats, and she makes a big batch that lasts for a couple of days. She likes the oatmeal thick and loaded with fresh berries. The heat from the oats warms the berries so they melt in your mouth, and the thick oats cool quickly with a splash of cold milk so her family doesn't have to wait as long to eat. I'm sure you'll enjoy it as much as they do!

2 tablespoons (28 g) unsalted butter

2 cups (352 g) steel cut oats

6½ cups (1.5 L) water

½ cup (120 ml) heavy cream

¼ cup (60 g) packed light brown sugar

¼ cup (21.25 g) dried cranberries

¼ teaspoon salt

¼ cup (44 g) chia seeds

1 teaspoon vanilla extract

1½ cups (255 g) fresh berries (raspberries, blackberries, blueberries, or sliced strawberries)

Sliced almonds, for garnish

Milk, for serving

—

Serves 8

Select Simmer/Sauté and melt the butter in the pressure cooking pot. Add the oats. Toast for about 3 minutes, stirring constantly, until they smell nutty. Stir in the water, heavy cream, brown sugar, cranberries, and salt. Lock the lid in place. Select High Pressure and 10 minutes cook time.

When the cook time ends, turn off the pressure cooker. Let the pressure release naturally for 10 minutes and finish with a quick pressure release. When the valve drops, carefully remove the lid. Stir in the chia seeds and vanilla. Cover and let sit for 5 minutes until the oats reach your desired thickness. Top with the berries, and finish with a sprinkle of sliced almonds and a splash of milk.

> **TIP**
>
> Chia seeds have a mild nutty flavor and are a good source of protein. If you don't have them on hand, omit them and reduce the water.

Carrot Cake Steel Cut Oats

The flavors of the classic dessert in a hearty, heart-healthy breakfast.

1 tablespoon (14 g) unsalted butter

1 cup (176 g) steel cut oats

1 quart (946 ml) water

1 cup (110 g) grated carrots

3 tablespoons (60 g) pure maple syrup, plus more for serving

2 teaspoons ground cinnamon

1 teaspoon pumpkin pie spice

¼ teaspoon salt

¾ cup (110 g) raisins, plus more for serving

¼ cup (44 g) chia seeds

Chopped nuts, for serving

Milk, for serving

—
Serves 6

Select Simmer/Sauté and add the butter to the pressure cooking pot to melt. Add the oats. Toast for about 3 minutes, stirring constantly, until they smell nutty. Stir in the water, carrots, maple syrup, cinnamon, pumpkin pie spice, and salt. Lock the lid in place. Select High Pressure and 10 minutes cook time.

When the cook time ends, turn off the pressure cooker. Let the pressure release naturally for 10 minutes and finish with a quick pressure release. When the valve drops, carefully remove the lid. Stir in the raisins and chia seeds. Cover and let sit for 5 to 10 minutes until the oats reach your desired thickness. Serve topped with more raisins, maple syrup, chopped nuts, and milk.

TIP

If you don't have pumpkin pie spice, make your own: Combine ½ teaspoon ground cinnamon, ¼ teaspoon ground ginger, ¼ teaspoon ground nutmeg, and ⅛ teaspoon ground cloves.

Apple-Cinnamon Oatmeal

Old-fashioned oatmeal made in the pressure cooker is perfect for busy mornings. This dish is ready in no time, giving you the chance to enjoy your coffee before your day starts!

1 tablespoon (14 g) unsalted butter

2 cups (470 ml) water

1 cup (156 g) old-fashioned oats

1 cup (150 g) diced apple

2 tablespoons (30 g) packed light brown sugar

¼ teaspoon ground cinnamon

¼ teaspoon salt

—

Serves 2 to 3

Select Simmer/Sauté and melt the butter in the pressure cooking pot. Add the water, oats, apple, brown sugar, cinnamon, and salt. Lock the lid in place. Select High Pressure and 1 minute cook time.

When the cook time ends, turn off the pressure cooker. Let the pressure release naturally for 10 minutes and finish with a quick pressure release. When the valve drops, carefully remove the lid. Stir the oatmeal and serve hot with your choice of toppings.

TIP

I top my oatmeal with sliced almonds, extra brown sugar, and a splash of milk around the edges to cool it down. Oatmeal really is a blank slate—change up the toppings to fit what you have on hand.

Oatmeal for One

On weekdays in our busy home, everyone fixes their own breakfast. On cold, snowy days, I crave a hearty, warm breakfast that will keep me going until lunch. Making a single batch of oatmeal in the pressure cooker doesn't save a lot of time, but you can cook the oatmeal in the same bowl you'll eat it in, and you can leave the kitchen while it cooks without worrying that your oatmeal will boil over.

½ cup (78 g) old-fashioned oats

1 cup (235 ml) water

Pinch salt

—

Serves 1

In a small, deep, ovenproof bowl with at least a 2-cup (470 ml) capacity, stir together the oats, water, and salt. Put a trivet in the pressure cooking pot and add 1 cup (235 ml) water. Place the bowl on the trivet. Lock the lid in place. Select High Pressure and 2 minutes cook time.

When the cook time ends, turn off the pressure cooker. Let the pressure release naturally for 5 minutes and finish with a quick pressure release. When the valve drops, carefully remove the lid. Stir the oatmeal and serve hot with your choice of toppings.

TIP

This oatmeal has no added sugar, allowing you to control just how much sweetness you need to start your day.

Cherry-Orange Breakfast Quinoa

This light, fluffy quinoa combines a rise-and-shine orange flavor with tart cherries in a quick fiber- and protein-packed breakfast that will keep you full all morning.

2¼ cups (540 ml) water

1½ cups (276 g) uncooked quinoa, well rinsed

2 tablespoons (24 g) sugar

Juice of 1 orange

Zest of 1 orange

¼ teaspoon salt

½ cup (80 g) dried cherries, chopped

Milk, sliced almonds, and sugar, for topping

—

Serves 6

In the pressure cooking pot, combine the water, quinoa, sugar, orange juice, orange zest, and salt. Lock the lid in place. Select High Pressure and 1 minute cook time.

When the cook time ends, turn off the pressure cooker. Let the pressure release naturally for 10 minutes and finish with a quick pressure release. When the valve drops, carefully remove the lid. Fluff the quinoa with a fork and stir in the cherries. Serve hot topped with milk, sliced almonds, and more sugar, if desired.

TIP

I freeze cooked quinoa in individual portions in freezer bags so I can just grab and go on busy mornings.

Crustless Ham and Cheese Quiche

No crust plus your pressure cooker equals no fuss. This crustless quiche is loaded with ham, cheese, and scallions and cooks up light and fluffy.

6 large eggs, well beaten

½ cup (120 ml) milk

⅛ teaspoon salt

⅛ teaspoon freshly ground black pepper

1 cup (150 g) diced ham

2 large scallions, white and green parts, chopped

1 cup (115 g) shredded Cheddar cheese

¼ cup (20 g) shredded Parmesan cheese

—

Serves 4 to 6

Put a metal trivet in the bottom of the pressure cooking pot and add 1½ cups (360 ml) water.

In a large bowl, whisk the eggs, milk, salt, and pepper. Set aside.

Spray a 7-inch (18 cm) round cake pan or 1½-quart (1.4 L) ovenproof dish with nonstick cooking spray. Add the ham, scallions, and Cheddar and mix well. Pour the eggs over the ham mixture and stir to combine. Sprinkle the top with Parmesan. Use a sling to place the dish on the trivet. Lock the lid in place. Select High Pressure and 20 minutes cook time.

When the cook time ends, turn off the pressure cooker. Let the pressure release naturally for 10 minutes and finish with a quick pressure release. When the valve drops, carefully remove the lid. Lift out the dish. You can serve this immediately or pop the dish in a preheated broiler and broil until the top is lightly browned.

> **TIP**
>
> This recipe is easy to customize to your taste. Load this quiche with sausage, bacon, and ham for a hearty meat lover's special or substitute roasted vegetables for the ham for a healthy start to your day.

Hash Brown Breakfast Casserole

When you crave something a little more substantial to start the day, this easy one-pot hash brown breakfast casserole is sure to become a favorite.

3 slices bacon, coarsely chopped

½ cup (80 g) chopped onion

2 cups (420 g) frozen hash brown potatoes

8 large eggs

¼ cup (60 ml) milk

¼ teaspoon salt

¼ teaspoon freshly ground black pepper

¾ cup (90 g) shredded Cheddar cheese, divided

—
Serves 6

TIP

My family prefers crisp bacon. If the bacon doesn't brown evenly in the pressure cooking pot, after I transfer it to a plate, I put it in the microwave for 30 seconds to crisp up.

Spray a 7-inch (18 cm) round cake pan or a 1½-quart (1.4 L) baking dish with nonstick cooking spray.

Select Browning/Sauté and add the bacon to the pressure cooking pot. Fry for about 5 minutes until crisp, stirring occasionally. Transfer the bacon to a paper towel–lined plate, leaving the bacon fat in the pot. Add the onion. Sauté for 3 minutes, stirring frequently. Transfer the onion to the prepared pan and add the cooked bacon and hash browns. Set aside.

In a large bowl, whisk the eggs, milk, salt, and pepper. Mix in ½ cup (60 g) Cheddar. Pour the egg mixture over the hash browns and bacon and stir to combine. Sprinkle the remaining ¼ cup (30 g) Cheddar on top—do not stir.

Put a trivet in the bottom of the pressure cooking pot and add 1 cup (235 ml) water. (You don't need to clean the pot after cooking the onion. The water will help clean it as the casserole cooks.) Center the dish on a sling and carefully lower it onto the trivet. Lock the lid in place. Select High Pressure and 20 minutes cook time.

When the cook time ends, turn off the pressure cooker. Let the pressure release naturally for 10 minutes and finish with a quick pressure release. When the valve drops, carefully remove the lid and use a paper towel to blot up any water that collected on the casserole. If desired, brown the cheese under a preheated broiler for a few minutes before serving.

Mexican Breakfast Casserole

Spice up your morning with this easy, meaty, cheesy, Mexican-inspired casserole. The tortillas dissolve into the eggs, giving the casserole body and a great corn flavor.

4 (5 inches, or 13 cm) corn tortillas, torn into bite-size pieces

1 tablespoon (15 ml) vegetable oil

1 pound (454 g) ground chorizo or Italian sausage

8 large eggs

⅓ cup (78 ml) milk

½ teaspoon salt

¼ teaspoon freshly ground black pepper

1 can (4 oz, or 113 g) diced mild green chilies

½ cup (59 g) crumbled queso fresco

3 scallions, white and green parts, chopped

½ cup (58 g) shredded Cheddar cheese

—
Serves 6

TIP

Queso fresco is a fresh-tasting, mild Mexican cheese that's easily crumbled. If it's not available in your area, substitute a shredded Mexican cheese blend.

Spray a 7-inch (18 cm) round cake pan with a generous amount of nonstick cooking spray. Place the tortilla pieces in the prepared pan.

Select Browning/Sauté to preheat the pressure cooking pot. When hot, add the vegetable oil and chorizo. Cook for about 5 minutes, stirring frequently, until brown and crumbled. Use a slotted spoon to transfer to a paper towel–lined plate. Set aside. Drain any excess fat from the pot.

In a large bowl, whisk the eggs, milk, salt, and pepper. Stir in the green chilies, queso fresco, scallions, and browned chorizo. Pour the egg mixture into the prepared pan and stir to combine. Sprinkle the top with Cheddar.

Put a trivet in the bottom of the pressure cooking pot and add 1 cup (235 ml) water. Center the pan on a sling and carefully lower it onto the trivet. Lock the lid in place. Select High Pressure and 25 minutes cook time.

When the cook time ends, turn off the pressure cooker. Let the pressure release naturally for 10 minutes and finish with a quick pressure release. When the valve drops, carefully remove the lid. Lift out the dish. If desired, broil until the cheese is lightly browned.

Maple-Almond-Raisin Breakfast Risotto

This breakfast risotto is similar to rice pudding but has less fat and sugar. You may find yourself eating it for dessert as well.

2 tablespoons (28 g) unsalted butter

1½ cups (288 g) arborio rice

1 quart (946 ml) unsweetened almond milk, plus more as needed

½ cup (75 g) raisins

¼ cup (80 g) pure maple syrup, plus more for serving

¼ cup (60 g) packed light brown sugar

1 teaspoon vanilla extract

½ teaspoon ground cinnamon

¼ teaspoon salt

Sliced almonds, for serving

—

Serves 6

Select Browning/Sauté and melt the butter in the pressure cooking pot. Stir in the rice. Cook for about 3 minutes, stirring frequently, until fragrant. Stir in the almond milk, raisins, maple syrup, brown sugar, vanilla, cinnamon, and salt. Lock the lid in place. Select High Pressure and 6 minutes cook time.

When the cook time ends, turn off the pressure cooker. Let the pressure release naturally for 5 minutes and finish with a quick pressure release. When the valve drops, carefully remove the lid. Stir the mixture. Add more almond milk, if needed, to achieve a creamy consistency. Serve topped with maple syrup, sliced almonds, and a splash of almond milk.

TIP

This dish tastes great the next day as well. Add more almond milk before you rewarm it to get that creamy consistency back.

Parmesan, Spinach, and Tomato Egg Muffins

These egg muffins are like crustless mini quiches. This colorful spinach-tomato version is loaded with healthy veggies and makes a great meal on the run.

8 large eggs

¼ cup (60 ml) milk

¼ teaspoon salt

⅛ teaspoon freshly ground black pepper

1 cup (30 g) fresh baby spinach, chopped

½ cup (90 g) diced seeded tomato

2 scallions, white and green parts, sliced

⅓ cup (26.6 g) shredded Parmesan cheese

—
Serves 6

Spray 6 (6-ounce, or 170 g) ovenproof custard cups with nonstick cooking spray.

In a large bowl, whisk the eggs, milk, salt, and pepper until just blended. Evenly divide the spinach, tomato, and scallions among the custard cups. Pour the egg mixture over the veggies. Sprinkle the Parmesan over each.

Pour 1 cup (235 ml) water into the pressure cooking pot and place a trivet in the bottom. Place 3 custard cups on the trivet and place a second trivet on top. Place the remaining 3 cups on it. Lock the lid in place. Select High Pressure and 6 minutes cook time.

When the cook time ends, turn off the pressure cooker. Let the pressure release naturally for 5 minutes and finish with a quick pressure release. When the valve drops, carefully open the lid and remove the cups.

TIP

These keep for 1 week in the refrigerator, and they also freeze well. To reheat, microwave on high power for about 30 seconds.

CHAPTER 2

Sandwiches, Wraps, Tacos, and More

Sandwiches (and all their variations) aren't just for lunch—on a busy day, a sandwich is the perfect quick-to-make, quick-to-eat dinner. With your electric pressure cooker, you can make the sandwich fillings ahead of time and freeze them in single-serve or family-size portions.

Asian Chicken Lettuce Wraps

Meet my easy pressure cooker version of the popular restaurant lettuce wraps. The crunchy vegetables and pop of color from the scallions and carrots will have your family asking for this again and again.

1 tablespoon (15 ml) vegetable oil

1½ pounds (680 g) ground chicken

3 cloves garlic, minced

1 cup (235 ml) reduced-sodium chicken broth

½ cup (120 ml) hoisin sauce

¼ cup (60 ml) low-sodium soy sauce

1 teaspoon chili-garlic sauce, plus more for serving

½ cup (98 g) white rice

1 can (8 oz, or 227 g) sliced water chestnuts, drained and diced

1 tablespoon (8 g) cornstarch

1 tablespoon (15 ml) cold water

1 cup (130 g) frozen diced carrots, thawed

3 scallions, white and green parts, sliced

2 heads butter lettuce, for serving

—
Serves 6

Select Browning/Sauté to preheat the pressure cooking pot. When hot, add the vegetable oil and chicken. Cook for about 5 minutes, crumbling with a spoon, until browned. Add the garlic and cook for 1 minute more, stirring frequently. Stir in the chicken broth, hoisin sauce, soy sauce, and chili-garlic sauce. Stir in the rice and water chestnuts. Lock the lid in place. Select High Pressure and 4 minutes cook time.

When the cook time ends, turn off the pressure cooker. Let the pressure release naturally for 10 minutes and finish with a quick pressure release. When the valve drops, carefully remove the lid.

In a small bowl, whisk the cornstarch and cold water until smooth. Add the slurry to the pot. Select Simmer/Sauté and cook, stirring constantly, until the sauce reaches your desired thickness. Stir in the carrots and scallions. Serve wrapped in lettuce leaves topped with more chili-garlic sauce or Sriracha, if desired.

> **TIP**
>
> If you're unable to find butter lettuce, Boston and Bibb lettuce are close substitutes. In a pinch, iceberg or romaine lettuce can also work, or substitute corn or flour tortillas and make Asian chicken tacos.

Buffalo Chicken Tender Sandwiches with Blue Cheese Sauce

The blue cheese sauce cools the heat from the spicy buffalo chicken. If you're a fan of buffalo chicken wings, I know you'll cheer for this easy-to-make sandwich.

For Buffalo Chicken:

½ cup (120 ml) water

2 tablespoons (30 ml) hot sauce

12 chicken tenders, frozen or fresh

4 sub rolls, split and toasted

Romaine or iceberg lettuce leaves, for serving

1 small red onion, thinly sliced

For Blue Cheese Sauce:

⅓ cup (75 g) mayonnaise

⅓ cup (75 g) sour cream

1 tablespoon (15 ml) lemon juice

Pinch salt and freshly ground black pepper

⅓ cup (40 g) blue cheese, crumbled

—
Serves 4

TO MAKE THE BUFFALO CHICKEN: Add the water and hot sauce to the pressure cooking pot and stir to combine. Add the chicken tenders. Lock the lid in place. Select High Pressure and 2 minutes cook time.

When the cook time ends, turn off the pressure cooker. Let the pressure release naturally for 5 minutes and finish with a quick pressure release. When the valve drops, carefully remove the lid. Use a slotted spoon to transfer the chicken to a plate. Shred the chicken using 2 forks and return it to the liquid in the cooking pot. Select Simmer/Sauté. Cook for about 5 minutes, uncovered and stirring occasionally, until all the liquid is absorbed or evaporates.

TO MAKE THE BLUE CHEESE SAUCE: In a small bowl, whisk the mayonnaise, sour cream, lemon juice, and salt and pepper, until smooth. Stir in the blue cheese.

TO MAKE THE SANDWICHES: Place a scoop of shredded chicken on the bottom of the sub roll and top with lettuce and red onion. Spread the top roll with blue cheese sauce and place it on top of the sandwich. Serve any remaining blue cheese sauce for dipping, if desired.

TIP

I prefer Frank's RedHot sauce, but feel free to substitute your favorite.

Greek Tacos

This delightful Greek version of tacos is made with tender chunks of seasoned pork braised in herbs and lemon juice, served on warm pita bread with lettuce, tomatoes, and cool, creamy tzatziki sauce.

For Pork:

1 teaspoon dried marjoram

½ teaspoon salt

¼ teaspoon freshly ground black pepper

2 tablespoons (30 ml) olive oil

4 pounds (1.8 kg) boneless pork shoulder, trimmed and cut into 1-inch (2.5 cm) cubes

½ cup (120 ml) fresh lemon juice

¼ cup (60 ml) water

Pita bread, diced tomato, and lettuce, for serving

For Tzatziki Sauce:

1 small cucumber, peeled, seeded, and shredded

¼ teaspoon salt

1 cup (230 g) plain Greek yogurt

1 tablespoon (15 ml) fresh lemon juice

1 teaspoon dried dill weed

1 clove garlic, minced or pressed

⅛ teaspoon freshly ground black pepper

—

Serves 8

TO MAKE THE PORK: In a small bowl, stir together the marjoram, salt, pepper, and olive oil. Rub this paste all over the cubed pork. Add the lemon juice and water to the pressure cooking pot. Place the pork in the pot. Lock the lid in place. Select High Pressure and 25 minutes cook time.

TO MAKE THE TZATZIKI SAUCE: While the pork cooks, in a fine-mesh strainer, toss the cucumber with the salt. Let the cucumber drain for 15 minutes over a bowl or the sink to remove excess water. In a medium-size bowl, stir together the drained cucumber, yogurt, lemon juice, dill weed, garlic, and pepper until well combined.

When the cook time ends, turn off the pressure cooker. Let the pressure release naturally for 10 minutes and finish with a quick pressure release. When the valve drops, carefully remove the lid. Using a slotted spoon, transfer the meat to a serving dish. Serve on pita with diced tomatoes, shredded lettuce, and tzatziki sauce.

TIP

This Greek taco meat freezes very well. Freeze in individual portions for quick, easy meals.

Carnitas Street Tacos

I have a favorite taqueria that serves upscale little street tacos with pretty pink pickled onions on top. The pickled onions add color, a burst of flavor, and a nice crunch to the taco—and they're easy to make.

For Pickled Onions:

1 small red onion, thinly sliced and quartered

1 cup (235 ml) hot water

½ cup (120 ml) apple cider vinegar

1 tablespoon (12 g) sugar

1 teaspoon salt

⅛ teaspoon red pepper flakes

For Tacos:

1 tablespoon (3 g) dried oregano

2 teaspoons ground cumin

2 teaspoons salt

1 teaspoon freshly ground black pepper

2 tablespoons (30 ml) olive oil

6 pounds (2.7 kg) boneless pork shoulder, trimmed and cut into 4 equal pieces

1 cup (235 ml) fresh orange juice (from about 2 large oranges)

2 onions, quartered

8 cloves garlic, smashed

2 jalapeño peppers, seeded, ribbed, and chopped

Small corn tortillas, queso fresco, fresh cilantro, lime juice, and sour cream, for serving

—

Serves 6

TO MAKE THE PICKLED ONIONS: In a small bowl, combine the red onion and hot water. Let soak for 1 minute. Drain. In a pint-size (470 ml) Mason jar, whisk the cider vinegar, sugar, and salt until dissolved. Add the red pepper flakes and red onion to the jar. Let sit at room temperature for 1 hour. Drain before using.

TO MAKE THE TACOS: In a small bowl, stir together the oregano, cumin, salt, pepper, and olive oil. Rub this paste over the pork pieces. In the pressure cooking pot, stir together the orange juice, onions, garlic, and jalapeños. Add the pork to the pot. Lock the lid in place. Select High Pressure and 50 minutes cook time.

When the cook time ends, turn off the pressure cooker. Let the pressure release naturally for 10 minutes and finish with a quick pressure release. When the valve drops, carefully remove the lid. Using a large fork or slotted spoon, carefully transfer the meat to a large platter and shred it with 2 forks. Discard any excess fat as you shred. Strain the juices in the cooking pot and set aside.

Serve immediately or crisp the pork before serving. To crisp, preheat the broiler. Line a rimmed baking sheet with aluminum foil and spread the pork in a single layer. Broil for 3 to 5 minutes, or until the edges of the pork start to brown and crisp.

Place the shredded pork in a serving bowl and ladle ½ cup (120 ml) reserved cooking liquid over the pork. Serve in warmed tortillas topped with the pickled red onions. Finish with queso fresco, chopped fresh cilantro leaves, a squeeze of lime juice, and sour cream, if desired.

TIP

Make life easier before a big get-together. Prepare the taco meat early in the morning or even a day ahead and reheat it in the pressure cooker with a little reserved cooking liquid.

Steak and Cheddar Sandwiches

A classic hot beef and Cheddar sandwich gets kicked up a notch with steak. Don't skip the hot sauce in the cheese sauce—it doesn't add much heat, but it does add a ton of flavor.

For Steak:

1 to 3 tablespoons (15 to 45 ml) vegetable oil, divided

2 pounds (907 g) boneless beef sirloin steak, sliced against the grain into ¼-inch-thick (0.6 cm) slices

½ cup (120 ml) reduced-sodium beef broth

½ teaspoon garlic powder

½ teaspoon salt

½ teaspoon freshly ground black pepper

8 onion hamburger buns, toasted

For Cheese Sauce:

2 tablespoons (28 g) unsalted butter

2 tablespoons (14 g) all-purpose flour

1 cup (235 ml) milk

2 teaspoons hot sauce (I use Frank's RedHot)

¼ teaspoon salt

1½ cups (173 g) shredded Cheddar cheese

—

Serves 4 to 6

TO MAKE THE STEAK: Add 1 tablespoon (15 ml) vegetable oil to the pressure cooking pot and quickly brown the beef strips on one side. Work in batches, adding more vegetable oil as needed, until all the meat is browned on one side. Transfer the meat to a plate when browned.

Add the beef broth, garlic powder, salt, and pepper to the cooking pot and stir to combine. Return the browned beef to the pot. Lock the lid in place. Select High Pressure and 12 minutes cook time.

TO MAKE THE CHEESE SAUCE: While the beef cooks, in a medium-size saucepan over medium heat, melt the butter. Sprinkle in the flour and cook until bubbling. Gradually whisk in the milk a little at a time until the sauce is smooth and thick. Whisk in the hot sauce and salt. Add the Cheddar a handful at a time and stir until melted and smooth. Remove from the heat.

When the cook time ends, turn off the pressure cooker. Use a quick pressure release. When the valve drops, carefully remove the lid. To serve, top each bun with a mound of beef slices and ladle cheese sauce on top.

TIP

Lightly butter the hamburger buns and toast in a 350°F (180°C, or gas mark 4) oven for about 5 minutes until golden-brown.

Barbecue Beef Brisket Tacos

These tacos are a fusion of Mexican and barbecue flavors. I first tasted this fantastic flavor combination at a neighborhood street fair, where a local barbecue restaurant serves this as their Wednesday special. I couldn't resist re-creating these at home in the pressure cooker, so now I can have them any day of the week.

For Coleslaw:

½ cup (115 g) mayonnaise

2 tablespoons (30 ml) apple cider vinegar

2 teaspoons sugar

¼ teaspoon salt

4 cups (280 g) coleslaw mix

For Filling:

½ cup (120 ml) water

2 tablespoons (15 g) chili powder

1 tablespoon (18 g) salt

1 teaspoon freshly ground black pepper

1 teaspoon garlic powder

½ teaspoon cayenne pepper

3 pounds (1.36 kg) flat-cut beef brisket, halved equally

8 (4 inches, or 10 cm) flour tortillas

½ cup (125 g) barbecue sauce, for serving

—

Serves 8

TO MAKE THE COLESLAW: In a large bowl, stir together the mayonnaise, cider vinegar, sugar, and salt. Add the coleslaw mix and stir until well combined. Refrigerate until serving.

TO MAKE THE FILLING: In the pressure cooking pot, stir together the water, chili powder, salt, pepper, garlic powder, and cayenne. Add the brisket, fat-side up. Lock the lid in place. Select High Pressure and 60 minutes cook time.

When the cook time ends, turn off the pressure cooker. Let the pressure release naturally for 10 minutes and finish with a quick pressure release. When the valve drops, carefully remove the lid. Transfer the brisket to a rimmed baking sheet and shred the meat.

To serve, top the tortillas with 2 tablespoons (28 g) brisket and a drizzle of barbecue sauce, then finish with the coleslaw.

> **TIP**
>
> If you prefer, buy prepared coleslaw at the deli counter instead of making your own.

Cheesy Baked Chicken Taquitos

Taquitos are small, rolled tacos that are often deep-fried. I've created a baked version filled with a chicken and cheese filling that comes together quickly in the pressure cooker.

½ cup (120 ml) water

¼ cup (32 g) green salsa, plus more for serving

1 teaspoon chili powder

½ teaspoon onion powder

½ teaspoon ground cumin

½ teaspoon garlic powder

½ teaspoon salt

¼ teaspoon freshly ground black pepper

2 large chicken breasts, fresh or frozen

1 tablespoon (15 ml) fresh lime juice

1 package (3 ounces, or 85 g) cream cheese, cubed

10 (6 inches, or 15 cm) flour tortillas

1½ cups (173 g) shredded Colby Jack cheese

3 tablespoons (3 g) fresh chopped cilantro leaves

2 scallions, white and green parts, chopped

Guacamole and sour cream, for serving

—
Serves 10

Preheat the oven to 400°F (200°C, or gas mark 6). Line a baking sheet with aluminum foil and lightly coat it with nonstick cooking spray.

In the pressure cooking pot, stir together the water, green salsa, chili powder, onion powder, cumin, garlic powder, salt, and pepper. Add the chicken. Lock the lid in place. Select High Pressure and 10 minutes cook time.

When the cook time ends, turn off the pressure cooker. Use a quick pressure release. When the valve drops, carefully remove the lid. Remove the chicken, shred it, and return it to the pot. Select Simmer/Sauté and cook uncovered for about 5 minutes, stirring occasionally, until all the liquid is absorbed. Stir in the lime juice. A little at a time, stir in the cream cheese until melted.

Divide the chicken mixture among the tortillas, placing it near the bottom. Top with the Colby Jack, cilantro, and scallions. Tightly roll the tortilla around the filling. Place each taquito, seam-side down, on the prepared baking sheet. Spray the tops with cooking spray. Bake for 10 to 15 minutes until crisp and golden-brown on the ends, turning seam-side up halfway through the baking time. Serve with guacamole, green salsa, and sour cream, if desired.

> **TIP**
>
> My family prefers flour tortillas, but corn tortillas work, too.

Shredded Barbecue Chicken Sandwiches

When you're craving pulled pork but need something quicker, these shredded barbecue chicken sandwiches are just the ticket.

2 cups (500 g) barbecue sauce, divided, plus more for serving

1 cup (235 ml) water

1 teaspoon liquid smoke

1 large onion, quartered

3 cloves garlic, smashed

4 large boneless skinless chicken breasts

8 sandwich rolls, toasted

—

Serves 8

In the pressure cooking pot, stir together 1 cup (250 g) barbecue sauce, the water, and liquid smoke. Add the onion, garlic, and chicken breasts. Lock the lid in place. Select High Pressure and 6 minutes cook time.

When the cook time ends, turn off the pressure cooker. Let the pressure release naturally for 5 minutes and finish with a quick pressure release. When the valve drops, carefully remove the lid. Transfer the chicken to a plate and shred it with 2 forks. Strain the cooking liquid, reserving ½ cup (120 ml).

Return the chicken to the cooking pot and add the remaining 1 cup (250 g) barbecue sauce and reserved cooking liquid. Stir to combine. Select Simmer/Sauté and bring the mixture to a simmer, stirring frequently. Serve on toasted rolls topped with barbecue sauce.

> **TIP**
>
> Toasting the rolls helps keep the sauce from making them soggy—so don't skip that step.

Three-Ingredient Pulled Pork

Pulled pork doesn't have to take all day. This easy pulled pork gives you the flavor of slow-cooked pulled pork in a fraction of the time—and with only three ingredients, you're out of the kitchen in a flash.

2 tablespoons (30 ml) vegetable oil

4 pounds (1.8 kg) boneless pork shoulder, trimmed and cut into 4 equal pieces

2 cups (500 g) barbecue sauce, divided, plus more for serving

½ cup (120 ml) water

8 sandwich rolls, toasted

—
Serves 8

Select Browning/Sauté and add the vegetable oil to the cooking pot. When the oil is hot, add 2 pieces of pork. Brown for about 3 minutes per side. When browned, transfer to a platter and repeat with the remaining 2 pieces.

Add 1 cup (250 g) barbecue sauce and ½ cup (120 ml) water to the cooking pot. Add the browned pork and any accumulated juices. Lock the lid in place. Select High Pressure and 60 minutes cook time.

When the cook time ends, turn off the pressure cooker. Use a natural pressure release. When the valve drops, carefully remove the lid. Carefully transfer the meat to a bowl and shred it with 2 forks, discarding any excess fat.

Strain the cooking liquid into a fat separator and reserve ½ cup (120 ml). Return the shredded pork to the cooking pot. Stir in the remaining 1 cup (250 g) barbecue sauce and reserved cooking liquid. Select Simmer/Sauté and bring to a simmer, stirring frequently. Serve on toasted rolls with more barbecue sauce, if desired.

> **TIP**
>
> I brown the roast to deepen the flavor a bit, but you can skip that step if you're in a hurry or feeling a bit lazy. Some days are like that.

Easy French Dip Sandwiches

French dip sandwiches don't get much easier than this! The meat cooks in an easy-to-make beef and onion broth that starts with a packet of dried onion soup mix, so there's not even any chopping to do.

1½ pounds (680 g) boneless beef top round roast, thinly sliced

1 can (14.5 fluid ounces, or 429 ml) reduced-sodium beef broth

1 packet dried onion soup mix

1 teaspoon finely crushed dried rosemary

½ teaspoon garlic powder

Butter, for the sub rolls

4 sub rolls, sliced lengthwise

8 slices of provolone cheese

—

Serves 4

In the pressure cooking pot, combine the beef, beef broth, onion soup mix, rosemary, and garlic powder. Lock the lid in place. Select High Pressure and 10 minutes cook time.

When the cook time ends, turn off the pressure cooker. Let the pressure release naturally for 10 minutes and finish with a quick pressure release. When the valve drops, carefully remove the lid.

Remove the meat from the broth. Strain the broth and skim off any fat. Butter and toast the sub rolls under a preheated broiler. Top each roll with meat and 2 slices of cheese. Broil again, just until the cheese melts and starts to bubble. Serve the broth in small cups for dipping.

TIP

I generally have the butcher slice meat for me; if you slice it yourself, put the roast in the freezer for about 30 minutes before slicing—meat is easier to slice when it's slightly frozen.

Sweet-and-Spicy Sloppy Joes

There's no need to buy sloppy joe sauce in a can when it's so easy and inexpensive to make your own from ingredients you probably already have in your cupboard.

2 pounds (907 g) lean ground beef

1 tablespoon (15 ml) vegetable oil

1 cup (160 g) diced onion

4 cloves garlic, finely chopped

1 can (28 ounces, or 794 g) crushed tomatoes in purée

1 cup (235 ml) water

1 tablespoon (15 g) packed light brown sugar

2 tablespoons (30 ml) Worcestershire sauce

2 teaspoons chili powder

1 teaspoon dry mustard

½ teaspoon salt

¼ teaspoon freshly ground black pepper

8 sandwich buns, toasted

Serves 8

Select Browning/Sauté. Brown the ground beef for about 5 minutes in the pressure cooking pot, stirring occasionally until the beef crumbles and is no longer pink. Transfer to a paper towel–lined plate. Drain any excess fat from the pot.

Add the vegetable oil and onion to the cooking pot. Sauté for about 3 minutes until tender. Add the garlic and sauté for 1 minute more. Stir in the tomatoes, water, brown sugar, Worcestershire sauce, chili powder, dry mustard, salt, and pepper. Add the browned beef and stir to combine. Lock the lid in place. Select High Pressure and 5 minutes cook time.

When the cook time ends, turn off the pressure cooker. Use a quick pressure release. When the valve drops, carefully remove the lid. Select Browning/Sauté and cook for about 5 minutes, stirring frequently, until the sauce reaches your desired thickness. Serve on toasted buns.

> **TIP**
>
> If your family likes green bell peppers, dice one and add it with the onion.

Beef and Bean Burritos

My daughter prefers her burritos with rice and beans as well as meat. This recipe lets you cook all three at the same time.

2 tablespoons (30 ml) vegetable oil, divided

1 pound (454 g) lean ground beef

1 cup (160 g) diced onion

3 cloves garlic, minced

2 teaspoons chili powder

1 teaspoon ground cumin

¼ teaspoon salt

1 can (15 ounces, or 425 g) black beans, drained and rinsed

1 cup (235 ml) reduced-sodium beef broth

½ cup (93 g) long-grain white rice

1 can (4 ounces, or 115 g) diced green chilies

Juice of 1 lime

2 tablespoons (2 g) chopped fresh cilantro leaves (optional)

6 burrito-size tortillas

Shredded Monterey Jack cheese, for serving

Salsa, for serving

—
Serves 6

Select Browning/Sauté to preheat the cooking pot. When hot, add 1 tablespoon (15 ml) vegetable oil and the ground beef. Cook for about 5 minutes, stirring frequently, until the beef is browned and crumbled. With a slotted spoon, transfer the beef to a paper towel–lined plate.

Add the remaining 1 tablespoon (15 ml) vegetable oil and onion to the cooking pot. Sauté for about 3 minutes, stirring occasionally, until the onion is tender. Add the garlic and cook for 1 minute more. Stir in the browned beef, chili powder, cumin, and salt. Sauté for 2 minutes. Add the black beans, beef broth, rice, and green chilies. Lock the lid in place. Select High Pressure and 3 minutes cook time.

When the cook time ends, turn off the pressure cooker. Let the pressure release naturally for 10 minutes and finish with a quick pressure release. When the valve drops, carefully remove the lid. Stir in the lime juice and cilantro.

Warm the tortillas in the microwave for 1 minute. Spread a small amount of the beef and bean mixture down the center of each tortilla and top with Monterey Jack and salsa. Fold the ends of the tortillas over and roll them up.

> **TIP**
>
> The spice level in this recipe is mild. If you like things a little hotter, double the chili powder.

CHAPTER 3

Soup's On

Soups made in the pressure cooker taste exactly like soups that simmer for hours on the stovetop. No need to serve your family soup from a can when you can have many homemade soups from your pressure cooker to the table in under 30 minutes.

Creamy Chicken and Wild Rice Soup

A rich, creamy chicken and wild rice soup loaded with chicken, long-grain and wild rice, carrots, onions, and celery. This warm, hearty soup is perfect for cold snowy days.

2 tablespoons (32 g) unsalted butter

1 cup (160 g) chopped onion

1 cup (130 g) diced carrots

1 cup (120 g) diced celery

2 large boneless skinless chicken breasts, diced into bite-sized pieces

2 cans (14.5 fluid ounces, or 429 ml, each) reduced-sodium chicken broth

1 package (6 ounces, or 170 g) Ben's Original Long-Grain and Wild Rice (discard seasoning packet)

—

Serves 6

Select Browning/Sauté and melt the butter in the pressure cooking pot. Add the onion, carrots, and celery. Sauté for about 5 minutes, stirring occasionally, until the vegetables are tender. Stir in the chicken, chicken broth, rice, parsley, salt, pepper, and red pepper flakes. Lock the lid in place. Select High Pressure and 5 minutes cook time.

When the cook time ends, turn off the pressure cooker. Let the pressure release naturally for 5 minutes and finish with a quick pressure release.

In a small bowl, whisk the cornstarch and cold water until smooth. Select Simmer/Sauté and add the slurry to the pot stirring constantly. Stir in the cream cheese until melted. Stir in the milk and half-and-half, heat through—do not bring to a boil—and serve.

TIP

My *Pressure Cooking Today* blog readers have had success substituting regular wild rice in this recipe instead of the long-grain wild rice blend.

Louisiana Gumbo

Gumbo is a Louisiana stew thickened with a flavorful roux and loaded with veggies, chicken, sausage, and seafood.

½ cup (120 ml) vegetable oil, divided

1 pound (454 g) Andouille sausage, halved lengthwise and cut into ¼-inch -thick (0.6 cm) slices

3 large boneless skinless chicken breasts

½ cup (56 g) all-purpose flour

1 large onion, diced

2 ribs celery, sliced

½ green bell pepper, chopped

4 cloves garlic, minced

5 cups (1.2 L) reduced-sodium chicken broth

1 can (14.5 ounces, or 411 g) diced tomatoes

2 cups (about 200 g) frozen sliced okra

1 tablespoon (15 ml) Worcestershire sauce

½ teaspoon cayenne pepper

8 ounces (227 g) small cooked shrimp, peeled and deveined

Salt and freshly ground black pepper, for seasoning

2 scallions, white and green parts, sliced, for garnish

—
Serves 6

Select Browning/Sauté to preheat the pressure cooking pot. Add ¼ cup (60 ml) vegetable oil and the sausage. Cook for about 3 minutes until browned. Transfer to a plate. Add the chicken. Cook for about 3 minutes per side to brown. Transfer to a cutting board and cut the chicken into bite-size pieces.

Add 2 tablespoons (30 ml) vegetable oil to the cooking pot and sprinkle the flour over the oil. Cook for about 10 minutes, stirring constantly, until the roux is medium to dark brown. Transfer to a bowl to cool.

Add the remaining 2 tablespoons (30 ml) vegetable oil to the cooking pot along with the onion, celery, and green bell pepper. Sauté for about 3 minutes, stirring occasionally, until the onion is tender. Add the garlic and cook for 1 minute more. Stir in the chicken broth, tomatoes, okra, Worcestershire sauce, cayenne, chicken, and sausage. Lock the lid in place. Select High Pressure and 4 minutes cook time.

When the cook time ends, turn off the pressure cooker. Let the pressure release naturally for 5 minutes and finish with a quick release. When the valve drops, carefully remove the lid. Select Simmer/Sauté and add the roux to the pot. Stir until the gumbo thickens. Add the shrimp and stir to combine. Season with salt and pepper to taste.

TIP

Gumbo is traditionally served over steamed or dirty rice.

Butternut Squash Soup with Chicken and Orzo

Smooth, creamy, and delicious! The black pepper and red pepper flakes give this soup a bit of heat, and the half-and-half gives it great body and beautiful color. It can stand on its own without the chicken and orzo, but I made the addition since my family prefers a heartier soup. On busy nights, I often use rotesserie chicken.

3 tablespoons (42 g) unsalted butter

½ cup (50 g) diced scallions, white and green parts, plus more for serving

½ cup (60 g) diced celery

½ cup (65 g) diced carrots

1 clove garlic, minced

2 cans (14.5 fluid ounces, or 429 ml, each) reduced-sodium chicken broth

1 can (14.5 ounces, or 411 g) diced tomatoes with juice

1½ pounds (680 g) butternut squash, peeled, cubed, and roasted

½ teaspoon Italian seasoning

¼ teaspoon freshly ground black pepper

⅛ teaspoon red pepper flakes

⅛ teaspoon freshly grated nutmeg

1 cup (140 g) cooked diced chicken

1 cup (about 8 ounces, or 227 g) orzo, cooked

½ cup (60 ml) half-and-half, plus more for serving

Scallions, for garnish

—
Serves 8

Select Browning/Sauté and melt the butter in the pressure cooking pot. Add the scallions, celery, and carrots. Sauté for about 3 minutes until tender. Add the garlic and cook for 1 minute more. Stir in the chicken broth, tomatoes, squash, Italian seasoning, pepper, red pepper flakes, and nutmeg. Lock the lid in place. Select High Pressure and 10 minutes cook time.

When the cook time ends, turn off the pressure cooker. Let the pressure release naturally for 10 minutes and finish with a quick pressure release. When the valve drops, carefully remove the lid. Use an immersion blender to purée the soup until very smooth. (You can also use a standard blender.)

Select Simmer/Sauté. Add the chicken, orzo, and ½ cup (120 ml) half-and-half. Heat for about 5 minutes until the chicken is heated through. Serve garnished with scallions and a swirl of half-and-half.

> **TIP**
>
> The soup has a richer flavor if you use roasted squash. Roast the cubed squash in a 400°F (200°C, or gas mark 6) oven on a baking sheet for about 20 minutes until it starts to brown and caramelize. If you're in a hurry or just don't want to turn on the oven, a reader of my blog, *Pressure Cooking Today*, suggested browning the squash in the pressure cooker with a little butter or oil, until it gets a nice caramelized coating.

Lighter Zuppa Toscana

I based this soup on an Italian restaurant's popular offering. This lighter pressure cooker version uses evaporated milk instead of heavy cream—without sacrificing flavor.

6 slices bacon, diced

1 pound (454 g) ground chicken sausage

1 tablespoon (14 g) unsalted butter

1 cup (160 g) diced onion

3 cloves garlic, minced or pressed

3 cans (14.5 fluid ounces, or 429 ml, each) reduced-sodium chicken broth, divided

½ teaspoon salt

½ teaspoon ground black pepper

⅛ teaspoon red pepper flakes

3 large russet potatoes, peeled and cubed

3 tablespoons (24 g) cornstarch

1 can (12 fluid ounces, or 355 ml) evaporated milk

1 cup (80 g) shredded Parmesan cheese, divided

2 cups (60 g) fresh spinach, chopped

—

Serves 8

Select Browning/Sauté and add the bacon to the pressure cooking pot. Fry for about 5 minutes until crisp, stirring frequently. Transfer to a paper towel–lined plate, leaving the bacon fat in the pot.

Add the sausage to the cooking pot. Cook for about 5 minutes until browned. Transfer to a second paper towel–lined plate.

Add the butter to the cooking pot to melt. Add the onion. Sauté for about 3 minutes, stirring occasionally, until tender. Add the garlic and cook for 1 minute more. Add 1 can (429 ml) chicken broth, the salt, pepper, and red pepper flakes. Put a steamer basket in the cooking pot. Add the potatoes. Lock the lid in place. Select High Pressure and 4 minutes cook time.

When the cook time ends, turn off the pressure cooker. Use a quick pressure release. When the valve drops, carefully remove the lid. Carefully remove the steamer basket with the potatoes from the cooking pot. Set aside. Add the remaining 2 cans (858 ml) chicken broth to the cooking pot.

In a small bowl, whisk the cornstarch in a little evaporated milk until smooth. Add the slurry to the pot along with the remaining evaporated milk. Select Simmer/Sauté and bring the mixture to a boil, stirring often. When the soup thickens, stir in ¾ cup (60 g) Parmesan, the spinach, browned sausage, potatoes, and half the crispy bacon. Serve topped with the remaining Parmesan and bacon.

TIP

When making soups, you don't have to add all the broth at once. The more broth you add, the longer the soup takes to come to pressure. Adding 1 can of broth while pressure cooking, and the remaining 2 cans after pressure cooking, speeds the process and keeps ingredients such as potatoes from being overcooked.

Chili con Carne

This thick, hearty chili is filled with tender bite-size pieces of beef, red beans, and green chilies and thickened with crushed tortilla chips. If you're a chili fanatic, this is a must-try recipe.

1 cup (250 g) dried red kidney beans

1 quart (946 ml) water

Salt and freshly ground black pepper, for seasoning

2 pounds (907 g) beef chuck, trimmed and cut in to 1-inch (2.5 cm) pieces

2 to 4 tablespoons (30 to 60 ml) vegetable oil, plus more as needed

1 cup (160 g) diced onion

2 cloves garlic, minced

1 can (14.5 fluid ounces, or 429 ml) reduced-sodium beef broth

1 can (14.5 ounces, or 411 g) crushed tomatoes

2 cans (4.5 ounces, or 128 g, each) mild green chilies

3 tablespoons (23 g) chili powder

2 tablespoons (32 g) tomato paste

1 teaspoon ground cumin

⅔ cup (about 20 g) finely crushed tortilla chips, plus more for serving

Shredded cheese, fresh cilantro, and sour cream, for serving

—

Serves 6

Add the beans and 1 quart (946 ml) water to the pressure cooking pot. Lock the lid in place. Select High Pressure and 1 minute cook time. When the cook time ends, turn off the pressure cooker. Let the beans soak in the pot for 1 hour. Drain and set aside.

Season the beef generously with salt and pepper. Select Browning/Sauté and add 2 tablespoons (30 ml) vegetable oil and the beef in small batches. Cook each batch for about 5 minutes to brown, adding more oil as needed and transferring to a plate when done. Continue in small batches, adding more oil as needed, until all the meat is browned.

Add more oil to the cooking pot along with the onion. Sauté for about 3 minutes until tender. Add the garlic and sauté for 1 minute more. Stir in the beef broth, tomatoes, green chilies, chili powder, tomato paste, and cumin. Stir in the browned beef and beans. Lock the lid in place. Select High Pressure and 25 minutes cook time.

When the cook time ends, turn off the pressure cooker. Let the pressure release naturally for 10 minutes and finish with a quick pressure release. When the valve drops, carefully remove the lid. Stir in the tortilla chips and let rest for 10 minutes, uncovered, to thicken. Serve topped with cheese, cilantro, sour cream, and more tortilla chips, as desired.

TIP

If you're short on time, replace the dried kidney beans with 2 cans (15 ounces, or 425 g, each) red kidney beans, drained and rinsed. Skip the first step and add the beans with the broth.

Minestrone Soup

A classic Italian soup loaded with veggies, beans, and pasta. This good-for-you soup is a great way to eat more veggies.

1 tablespoon (15 ml) olive oil

1 large onion, finely chopped

2 large carrots, diced

1 rib celery, diced

1 small zucchini, chopped

4 cloves garlic, minced

3 cans (14.5 fluid ounces, or 429 ml, each) reduced-sodium chicken broth, divided

2 cans (14 ounces, or 397 g, each) diced tomatoes

1 can (14 ounces, or 397 g) crushed tomatoes in purée

¾ cup (56 g) small shell pasta

1½ teaspoons Italian seasoning

1 teaspoon salt, plus more as needed

½ teaspoon freshly ground black pepper, plus more as needed

1 can (15 ounces, or 425 g) kidney beans, drained and rinsed

1 can (15 ounces, or 425 g) white navy beans or cannellini beans, drained and rinsed

1 cup (124 g) frozen cut green beans

2 cups (60 g) fresh baby spinach

Parmesan cheese, for serving

—
Serves 8

Select Browning/Sauté and add the olive oil to the pressure cooking pot. When the oil is hot, add the onion. Sauté for about 3 minutes, stirring occasionally, until the onion is tender. Add the carrots, celery, zucchini, and garlic. Cook for 3 minutes more, stirring occasionally. Stir in 2 cans chicken broth, the tomatoes, pasta, Italian seasoning, salt, and pepper. Stir in the kidney beans, white beans, and green beans. Lock the lid in place. Select High Pressure and 3 minutes cook time.

When the cook time ends, turn off the pressure cooker. Let the pressure release naturally for 5 minutes and finish with a quick pressure release. When the valve drops, carefully remove the lid. Stir in the remaining 1 can chicken broth and the spinach. Season with salt and pepper to taste. Serve topped with Parmesan.

TIP

Adding the third can of chicken broth after pressure cooking allows the soup to come to pressure faster, prevents overfilling the pot, and helps cool the soup so that you can eat it sooner.

Posole (Pork and Hominy Stew)

Hominy is simply dried corn kernels soaked in lime or lye until soft, swollen, and slightly chewy. If you haven't tried hominy yet, now is the time—it's delicious and a good source of fiber.

2 tablespoons (30 ml) vegetable oil, divided

1 teaspoon salt, plus more as needed

1¼ pounds (567 g) boneless pork shoulder, trimmed and cut into 4-inch (10 cm) pieces

1 medium-size white onion, chopped

4 cloves garlic, minced

2 tablespoons (15 g) chili powder

1 quart (940 ml) reduced-sodium chicken broth, divided

2 tablespoons (16 g) cornstarch

¼ cup (60 ml) cold water

2 cans (29 ounces, or 822 g, each) hominy, drained and rinsed

Diced avocado and lime wedges, for serving

—
Serves 6

Select Browning/Sauté and add 1 tablespoon (15 ml) vegetable oil to the cooking pot. When the oil is hot, season the pork with salt and add it to the cooking pot. Cook for about 5 minutes until browned on all sides. Transfer to a large bowl.

Add the remaining 1 tablespoon (15 ml) vegetable oil to the cooking pot. When the oil is hot, add the onion, garlic, and chili powder. Sauté for 4 minutes until soft. Stir in 2 cups (470 ml) chicken broth to deglaze the pot, scraping up any browned bits from the bottom with a wooden spoon. Add the remaining 2 cups (470 ml) chicken broth and the pork. Lock the lid in place. Select High Pressure and 30 minutes cook time.

When the cook time ends, turn off the pressure cooker. Let the pressure release naturally for 10 minutes and finish with a quick pressure release. When the valve drops, carefully remove the lid. Transfer the pork back to the large bowl and shred it using 2 forks.

In a small bowl, whisk the cornstarch and cold water until smooth. Add the slurry to the pot. Select Simmer/Sauté and stir until the broth thickens. Stir in the shredded pork and hominy. Season with salt to taste. Serve with avocado and lime.

> **TIP**
>
> Squeeze a bit of lime juice directly on the avocado after cutting to prevent browning.

Broccoli Cheese Soup

My family prefers soups with at least a little texture. So I adapted traditional creamy broccoli cheese soup by leaving pieces of broccoli and carrot in the soup, which also gives it a prettier color. You'll also be pleased at how quick this great-tasting soup is to make and serve!

2 tablespoons (28 g) unsalted butter

1 cup (160 g) diced onion

2 cloves garlic, minced

2 cans (14.5 fluid ounces, or 429 ml, each) reduced-sodium chicken broth

4 cups (284 g) bite-size broccoli florets

1 cup (110 g) matchstick carrots

½ teaspoon salt, plus more as needed

¼ teaspoon freshly ground black pepper, plus more as needed

⅛ teaspoon red pepper flakes

¼ cup (32 g) cornstarch

¼ cup (60 ml) cold water

2 cups (470 ml) half-and-half

2 cups (240 g) grated Cheddar cheese

—
Serves 6

Select Browning/Sauté to preheat the pressure cooking pot. Add the butter and onion. Sauté for about 3 minutes until tender. Add the garlic and sauté for 1 minute more. Stir in the chicken broth, broccoli, carrots, salt, pepper, and red pepper flakes. Lock the lid in place. Select High Pressure and 1 minute cook time.

When the cook time ends, turn off the pressure cooker. Use a quick pressure release. When the valve drops, carefully remove the lid.

In a small bowl, whisk the cornstarch and cold water until smooth. Select Simmer/Sauté and add the slurry to the pot, stirring constantly until the soup comes to a boil and thickens. Turn off the pressure cooker. Gradually stir in the half-and-half. Add the Cheddar a handful at a time, stirring until it melts. Season with salt and pepper to taste.

> **TIP**
>
> Substitute frozen chopped broccoli in this recipe, if you prefer, without changing the cook time.

Garden Fresh Tomato, Basil, and Parmesan Soup

Make this soup in the summer with fresh-from-the-garden (or farmers' market) tomatoes and basil. Made in the pressure cooker, you can have it ready to eat in under 30 minutes, and it's so much better than that stuff in a can.

3 tablespoons (42 g) unsalted butter

1 large onion, diced

2 ribs celery, diced

1 large carrot, diced

2 cloves garlic, minced or crushed

2 cans (14.5 fluid ounces, or 429 ml, each) reduced-sodium chicken broth

3 pounds (1.4 kg) fresh tomatoes, cored, peeled, and quartered

¼ cup (9 g) fresh basil leaves

1 tablespoon (16 g) tomato paste

1 teaspoon sugar

½ teaspoon salt

½ teaspoon freshly ground black pepper

½ cup (40 g) shredded Parmesan cheese

1 cup (235 ml) half-and-half

—

Serves 6

Select Browning/Sauté and melt the butter in the pressure cooking pot. Add the onion, celery, and carrot. Sauté for about 3 minutes until tender. Add the garlic and cook for 1 minute, stirring often. Stir in the chicken broth, tomatoes, basil, tomato paste, sugar, salt, and pepper. Lock the lid in place. Select High Pressure and 5 minutes cook time.

When the cook time ends, turn off the pressure cooker. Let the pressure release naturally for 5 minutes and finish with a quick pressure release. When the valve drops, carefully remove the lid. Use an immersion or standard blender to purée the soup until very smooth. Select Simmer/Sauté, stir in the Parmesan and half-and-half, and simmer until heated through—do not boil.

> **TIP**
>
> If garden-ripe tomatoes aren't available, substitute 2 cans (14.5 ounces, or 411 g, each) diced tomatoes.

Chunky Potato Cheese Soup

This perfect potato soup cooks the potatoes in the steamer basket above the onions, broth, and spices, which cooks them without breaking them down. The finished soup is smooth and creamy with firm chunks of potato.

2 tablespoons (28 g) unsalted butter

½ cup (80 g) chopped onion

2 cans (14.5 fluid ounces, or 429 ml, each) reduced-sodium chicken broth, divided

2 tablespoons (3 g) dried parsley

1 teaspoon salt

½ teaspoon freshly ground black pepper

⅛ teaspoon red pepper flakes

4 cups (440 g) peeled and cubed russet potatoes

2 tablespoons (16 g) cornstarch

2 tablespoons (30 ml) cold water

3 ounces (85 g) cream cheese, cubed

1 cup (120 g) shredded Cheddar cheese

2 cups (470 ml) half-and-half

1 cup (165 g) frozen corn

6 slices crisp-cooked bacon, crumbled

—

Serves 6

Select Browning/Sauté and melt the butter in the pressure cooking pot. Add the onion. Sauté for about 5 minutes, stirring occasionally, until tender. Stir in 1 can chicken broth, the parsley, salt, pepper, and red pepper flakes. Put a steamer basket in the pressure cooking pot. Add the potatoes. Lock the lid in place. Select High Pressure and 4 minutes cook time.

When the cook time ends, turn off the pressure cooker. Let the pressure release naturally for 5 minutes and finish with a quick pressure release. When the valve drops, carefully remove the lid. Remove the steamer basket with the potatoes from the cooking pot.

In a small bowl, whisk the cornstarch and cold water until smooth. Select Simmer/Sauté and add the slurry to the pot, stirring constantly until the soup thickens. Stir in the cream cheese and Cheddar until they melt. Add the remaining can of chicken broth, the half-and-half, corn, bacon, and cooked potatoes. Stir to combine and heat through—do not bring to a boil—then serve.

TIP

If you don't have a steamer basket, cook the potatoes directly in the broth. The potatoes may not hold their shape quite as well, but the flavor will still be amazing.

Rhode Island Clam Chowder

If you're a clam chowder aficionado looking for something lighter and healthier, this Rhode Island Clam Chowder is just the ticket. With a clear broth loaded with potatoes, celery, bacon, and fresh herbs, it's a great alternative to the creamier Boston clam chowder.

3 slices bacon, diced

1 cup (160 g) diced onion

2 ribs celery, diced

3 cloves garlic, minced or crushed

6 red potatoes, diced into bite-size pieces

4 cans (6.5 ounces, or 184 g, each) chopped clams with juice

2 cups (470 ml) reduced-sodium chicken broth

3 sprigs fresh thyme

2 bay leaves

Salt and freshly ground black pepper, for seasoning

Chopped parsley and oyster crackers, for serving

—

Serves 6

Select Browning/Sauté and add the bacon to the pressure cooking pot. Fry for about 5 minutes until crisp, stirring frequently. Transfer to a paper towel–lined plate, leaving the bacon fat in the pot.

Add the onion and celery to the cooking pot. Sauté for about 5 minutes, stirring occasionally, until tender. Add the garlic and cook for 1 minute more. Stir in the potatoes, clams, chicken broth, thyme, and bay leaves. Lock the lid in place. Select High Pressure and 3 minutes cook time.

When the cook time ends, turn off the pressure cooker. Use a quick pressure release. When the valve drops, carefully remove the lid. Remove and discard the bay leaves and thyme. Season with salt and pepper to taste. Serve topped with the bacon. Finish with chopped parsley and oyster crackers, if desired.

TIP

You can substitute 1 teaspoon dried thyme for the fresh thyme.

Creamy Red Lentil Soup

Lentils are high in fiber and protein, and the red lentils in this recipe give this delicious soup its pretty orange color.

2 tablespoons (30 ml) olive oil

1 cup (160 g) diced onion

1 cup (130 g) diced carrots

½ cup (60 g) diced celery

5 cloves garlic, minced

2 cans (14.5 ounces, or 411 g, each) fire-roasted diced tomatoes

1 quart (946 ml) reduced-sodium vegetable broth

2 cups (470 ml) water

1½ cups (288 g) red lentils, rinsed

1 teaspoon ground cumin

½ teaspoon dried thyme

1 teaspoon salt, plus more as needed

½ teaspoon freshly ground black pepper, plus more as needed

2 cups (60 g) fresh baby spinach, coarsely chopped

1 tablespoon (15 ml) red wine vinegar

Heavy cream, for serving

—
Serves 8

Select Browning/Sauté and add the olive oil to the pressure cooking pot. When the oil is hot, add the onion, carrots, and celery. Sauté for about 5 minutes until tender. Add the garlic and cook for 1 minute more. Stir in the tomatoes, vegetable broth, water, lentils, cumin, thyme, salt, and pepper. Lock the lid in place. Select High Pressure and 10 minutes cook time.

When the cook time ends, turn off the pressure cooker. Let the pressure release naturally for 10 minutes and finish with a quick pressure release. When the valve drops, carefully remove the lid. Transfer 2 cups (470 ml) soup to a large bowl. Use an immersion or regular blender to purée the soup until smooth. Stir in the reserved soup, spinach, and red wine vinegar. Select Simmer/Sauté and cook for just a few minutes until the spinach wilts. Season with additional salt and pepper, if needed. Ladle the soup into bowls and serve with a swirl of heavy cream.

> **TIP**
>
> Puréeing only part of the soup gives the soup a great texture and body. If you prefer a smoother soup, purée all of it.

Asian Chicken Noodle Soup

This fabulous soup features Asian-flavored chicken broth with cabbage, mushrooms, scallions, and fun-to-eat curly ramen noodles.

2 tablespoons (30 ml) vegetable oil

1 cup (130 g) diced carrots

4 cloves garlic, minced

1 teaspoon grated peeled fresh ginger

2 pounds (907 g) boneless skinless chicken tenders, frozen

3 cans (14.5 fluid ounces, or 429 ml, each) reduced-sodium chicken broth

3 tablespoons (45 ml) low-sodium soy sauce

2 tablespoons (30 ml) mirin (rice wine)

2 tablespoons (30 ml) rice vinegar

1 teaspoon Sriracha

1 tablespoon (15 ml) sesame oil

2 packages (3 ounces, or 85 g, each) dry ramen noodles (discard the seasoning packets)

3 cups (270 g) slightly packed chopped napa cabbage

6 ounces (170 g) cremini mushrooms, sliced

1 tablespoon (15 ml) fresh lime juice

3 scallions, white and green parts, sliced, for serving

—
Serves 6

Select Browning/Sauté and add the vegetable oil to the pressure cooking pot. When the oil is hot, add the carrots. Sauté for about 3 minutes, stirring occasionally, until tender. Add the garlic and ginger and sauté for 1 minute more. Stir in the chicken, chicken broth, soy sauce, mirin, rice vinegar, Sriracha, and sesame oil. Lock the lid in place. Select High Pressure and 2 minutes cook time.

When the cook time ends, turn off the pressure cooker. Use a quick pressure release. When the valve drops, carefully remove the lid. Use a slotted spoon and kitchen shears to cut the chicken tenders into bite-size pieces in the cooking pot. Break the ramen noodles in half and stir them into the soup. Stir in the cabbage and mushrooms. Lock the lid in place. Select High Pressure and 0 minutes cook time (see Tip).

When the cook time ends, turn off the pressure cooker. Use a quick pressure release. When the valve drops, carefully remove the lid. Stir with a fork to separate the noodles. Stir in the lime juice. Serve garnished with scallions.

> **TIP**
>
> Some pressure cookers let you select a cook time of 0 minutes, essentially bringing the pressure cooker to pressure and then switching to the Keep Warm setting as soon as pressure is achieved. If your pressure cooker doesn't offer this, select High Pressure and allow the pressure cooker to come to pressure. Cancel the cooking cycle once the pressure has been reached and the timer starts to count down.

Ratatouille Soup

Ratatouille is a French vegetable stew loaded with colorful, nutrient-rich ingredients. Puréeing half the soup gives this dish a creamy texture without adding any cream.

2 tablespoons (30 ml) olive oil

1 large onion, diced

4 cloves garlic, minced or pressed

2 cups (470 ml) reduced-sodium chicken broth or vegetable broth

1 can (28 ounces, or 794 g) crushed tomatoes

1 small eggplant, diced

1 small zucchini, diced

1 yellow bell pepper, diced

¼ cup (9 g) fresh basil leaves, chopped, plus more for serving

1 teaspoon Italian seasoning

1½ teaspoons salt, plus more as needed

½ teaspoon freshly ground black pepper, plus more as needed

¼ teaspoon red pepper flakes

Fresh basil, for serving

—
Serves 6

Select Browning/Sauté and add the olive oil to the pressure cooking pot. Add the onion. Sauté for about 3 minutes, stirring occasionally, until tender. Add the garlic and cook for 1 minute more. Stir in the chicken broth, tomatoes, eggplant, zucchini, yellow bell pepper, basil, Italian seasoning, salt, pepper, and red pepper flakes. Lock the lid in place. Select High Pressure and 2 minutes cook time.

When the cook time ends, turn off the pressure cooker. Let the pressure release naturally for 5 minutes and finish with a quick pressure release. When the valve drops, carefully remove the lid. Transfer 3 cups (705 ml) soup to a large bowl. Use an immersion or standard blender to purée the remaining soup until smooth. Stir in the reserved soup. Season with salt and pepper to taste. Serve garnished with fresh basil.

TIP

When an eggplant is small, the nutrient-rich skin is tender and can be left on when dicing.

Sue's Hearty Taco Soup

This recipe was adapted from a slow cooker recipe that is a family favorite of my next-door neighbor, Sue. Whenever she cooks it, she changes it up based on what she has on hand.

1 pound (454 g) lean ground beef

¼ cup (14 g) dried onion

1 package (1.3 ounces, or 36 g) taco seasoning mix

1 teaspoon chili powder

1 teaspoon salt

1 quart (946 ml) water

1 can (14.5 ounces, or 411 g) diced tomatoes

1 can (15 fluid ounces, or 444 ml) tomato sauce

2 cans (15 ounces, or 425 g, each) black beans, drained and rinsed

1 can (15 ounces, or 425 g) pinto beans, drained and rinsed

1 can (15 ounces, or 425 g) corn, with liquid

1 can (4 ounces, or 113 g) diced green chilies, with liquid

Corn chips, sour cream, and shredded cheese, for serving

—

Serves 6 to 8

Select Browning/Sauté to preheat the pressure cooking pot. When hot, add the ground beef. Cook for about 5 minutes, stirring frequently, until browned and crumbled. Stir in the onion, taco seasoning mix, chili powder, and salt. Add the water, tomatoes, tomato sauce, black beans, pinto beans, corn, and green chilies. Stir to combine. Lock the lid in place. Select High Pressure and 5 minutes cook time.

When the cook time ends, turn off the pressure cooker. Let the pressure release naturally for 10 minutes and finish with a quick pressure release. When the valve drops, carefully remove the lid. Serve topped with your favorite toppings, such as corn chips, sour cream, or shredded cheese.

TIP

If you don't use lean ground beef in this recipe, drain any excess fat from the pot before adding the onion and seasonings.

CHAPTER 4

Shortcut Dinners

*Readers of my blog, **Pressure Cooking Today**, have asked me why most pressure cooker recipes in cookbooks aren't like the super simple recipes they see in the infomercials selling electric pressure cookers. If you were drawn to the electric pressure cooker by the ease of using a few simple, premade ingredients to get you out of the kitchen fast, these recipes are for you.*

Anytime Spaghetti and Meatballs

I made several versions of this recipe trying to perfect it, and my boys came to love having leftover spaghetti and meatballs in the fridge for a quick lunch or late-night dinner. When I stopped testing the recipe, my son asked me to teach him to make it so that he could have it whenever he wanted.

2 tablespoons (30 ml) olive oil

3 cloves garlic, finely chopped

¼ teaspoon red pepper flakes

1 pound (454 g) fully cooked Italian-style meatballs (½-ounce, or 15 g, size)

1 teaspoon salt

1 package (1 pound, or 454 g) spaghetti, broken in half

1 to 1½ quarts (946 ml to 1.4 L) water

1 jar (28 fluid ounces, or 828 ml) marinara sauce

2 tablespoons (5 g) chopped fresh basil leaves, optional

Freshly grated Parmesan cheese, for serving

—

Serves 8

Select Browning/Sauté. Add the olive oil, garlic, and red pepper flakes to the pressure cooking pot. Sauté for 1 minute. Add the meatballs in an even layer on the bottom of the pot. Sprinkle with salt and top with the spaghetti. Pour in enough water to just cover the spaghetti—do not stir. Lock the lid in place. Select High Pressure and 4 minutes cook time.

When the cook time ends, turn off the pressure cooker. Use a quick pressure release, or, if necessary, use an intermittent pressure release. When the valve drops, carefully remove the lid. Check for excess water and remove it with a ladle. Stir in the sauce and fresh basil. Serve topped with Parmesan.

Ready-When-You-Are Spaghetti with Ragù

There are lots of tasty marinara sauces at the market, but it's harder to find a hearty ragù sauce with chunks of meat in it. Fortunately, it's easy to add your own meat to your favorite store-bought marinara and, in the pressure cooker, you can cook the pasta while you heat the sauce.

½ pound (227 g) ground beef or ground Italian sausage

½ teaspoon onion powder

½ teaspoon garlic powder

2½ teaspoons (15 g) salt, divided

¼ teaspoon freshly ground black pepper

5 cups (1.2 L) water, plus more as needed

2 tablespoons (30 ml) vegetable oil

1 package (1 pound, or 454 g) spaghetti, broken in half

1 jar (28 fluid ounces, or 828 ml) marinara sauce

2 tablespoons (5 g) chopped fresh basil, optional

Freshly grated Parmesan cheese, for serving

—

Serves 8

Select Browning/Sauté. Add the ground beef to the pressure cooking pot. Sprinkle in the onion powder, garlic powder, ½ teaspoon salt, and the pepper. Sauté for about 5 minutes, stirring occasionally, until the beef is browned and crumbled. Transfer to a paper towel–lined plate. Drain any excess fat from the pot.

Add the water, remaining 2 teaspoons (12 g) salt, vegetable oil, and spaghetti to the pot. If needed, add more water to just cover the spaghetti—do not stir. Place a rack directly on the spaghetti.

In a 7-inch (18 cm) round cake pan, combine the browned beef and marinara sauce. Use a sling to carefully place the pan on the rack. Lock the lid in place. Select High Pressure and 4 minutes cook time.

When the cook time ends, turn off the pressure cooker. Use a quick pressure release or, if necessary, use an intermittent pressure release. Remove the pan and rack from the cooking pot. Ladle off any excess water from the spaghetti. Pour the sauce into the cooking pot over the spaghetti, add the basil, and stir to combine. Serve topped with Parmesan.

TIP

Brown 1 pound (454 g) sausage and freeze half for a busy day.

Creamy Mashed Potatoes

Since I first made mashed potatoes in the pressure cooker, I have never cooked them on the stove again. Steaming the potatoes above the water gives them a better texture—and makes this dish faster and easier, since you don't have to worry about the water boiling over.

6 medium-size russet potatoes (about 2 pounds, or 907 g), peeled and quartered

¼ cup (56 g) unsalted butter, melted

½ to ¾ cup (120 to 175 ml) milk, warmed

Salt and freshly ground black pepper, for seasoning

—

Serves 6

Add 1 cup (235 ml) water to the pressure cooking pot. Put a steamer basket in the pot and place the potatoes in the basket. Lock the lid in place. Select High Pressure and 5 minutes cook time.

When the cook time ends, turn off the pressure cooker. Use a quick pressure release. When the valve drops, carefully remove the lid. Use a fork to test the potatoes. If needed, relock the lid and cook at High Pressure for a few minutes more. Transfer the potatoes to a large serving bowl. Use a potato masher to mash the potatoes until mostly smooth. Mash in the butter. Gradually stir in the milk. Season with salt and pepper to taste.

> **TIP**
>
> For extra-smooth and creamy mashed potatoes, my husband likes to use a ricer. Sometimes we also substitute heavy cream for the milk.

Barbecue Chicken Legs

This recipe is so quick and easy, you'll make it again and again, all summer long.

1 teaspoon chili powder

½ teaspoon salt

¼ teaspoon freshly ground black pepper

12 chicken legs

1 cup (250 g) barbecue sauce

—

Serves 6

In a small bowl, mix the chili powder, salt, and pepper. Place the chicken legs on a rimmed baking sheet and sprinkle with the seasoning.

Place a rack in the pressure cooking pot. Add 1 cup (235 ml) water and place the seasoned chicken legs on the rack, stacking them crosswise on top of each other. Lock the lid in place. Select High Pressure and 4 minutes cook time.

When the cook time ends, turn off the pressure cooker. Let the pressure release naturally for 10 minutes and finish with a quick pressure release. When the valve drops, carefully remove the lid. Remove the chicken legs to a rimmed baking sheet and coat with the barbecue sauce.

Preheat a grill to medium heat. Place the chicken on the grill and cook for 3 to 5 minutes per side until the sauce is caramelized and sticky. Baste with more sauce as desired. Alternatively, finish in a very hot oven or under the broiler, watching carefully to prevent burning.

> **TIP**
>
> Pressure cook the chicken legs early in the day, refrigerate them until you're ready to serve, and finish them on the grill to warm them and caramelize the sauce.

Pot Stickers with Spicy Orange Dipping Sauce

These pot stickers are perfect for a quick appetizer when guests are coming, or they can be part of an easy lunch or dinner any night of the week.

2 tablespoons (38 g) orange marmalade

1 tablespoon (15 g) packed light brown sugar

2 teaspoons low-sodium soy sauce

1 teaspoon rice wine vinegar

¼ teaspoon chili-garlic sauce

¼ teaspoon sesame oil

12 frozen pot stickers

—

Serves 4

In a small bowl, whisk the orange marmalade, brown sugar, soy sauce, vinegar, chili-garlic sauce, and sesame oil. Set aside until ready to serve.

Put a steamer basket in the pressure cooking pot and add 1 cup (235 ml) water. Spray the steamer basket with nonstick cooking spray. Add the pot stickers in a single layer. Lock the lid in place. Select High Pressure and 2 minutes cook time.

When the cook time ends, turn off the pressure cooker. Use a quick pressure release. When the valve drops, carefully remove the lid. Serve the pot stickers with the dipping sauce.

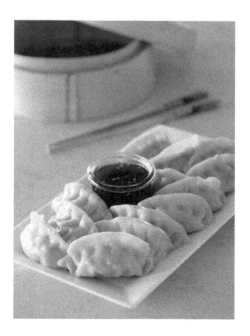

TIP

For a restaurant- quality look, brown the pot stickers after pressure cooking. Reduce the High Pressure cook time to 1 minute. After the quick pressure release, add 1 tablespoon (15 ml) vegetable oil to a preheated skillet and place the pot stickers in a single layer. Cook for about 1 minute until golden-brown.

Short-Order Buffalo Wings with Blue Cheese Dip

The pressure cooker makes short work of buffalo wings. Pressure cook them early and finish them under the broiler before the big game!

For Blue Cheese Dip:

½ cup (115 g) sour cream

½ cup (115 g) mayonnaise

½ cup (60 g) crumbled blue cheese

3 scallions, white and green parts, finely chopped

1 tablespoon (1 g) dried parsley

1 tablespoon (15 ml) lemon juice

¼ teaspoon garlic salt

¼ teaspoon ground black pepper

For Wings:

¼ cup (60 ml) water

1 cup (235 ml) Frank's RedHot Buffalo sauce, divided

1 tablespoon (8 g) paprika

3 pounds (1.4 kg) chicken wings, split at the joints

2 tablespoons (40 g) honey

—
Serves 6 to 8

TO MAKE THE BLUE CHEESE DIP: In a medium-size bowl, stir together the sour cream, mayonnaise, blue cheese, scallions, dried parsley, lemon juice, garlic salt, and pepper until well blended. Cover and refrigerate until ready to serve.

TO MAKE THE BUFFALO WINGS: In the pressure cooking pot, stir together the water, ¼ cup (60 ml) buffalo sauce, and paprika. Add the wings. Lock the lid in place. Select High Pressure and 6 minutes cook time.

When the cook time ends, turn off the pressure cooker. Let the pressure release naturally for 10 minutes and finish with a quick pressure release. When the valve drops, carefully remove the lid.

In a large bowl, mix the remaining ¾ cup (175 ml) buffalo sauce with the honey. Use a slotted spoon to remove the wings from the cooking pot and add them to the bowl. Stir to coat the wings with the sauce. Preheat the broiler.

Line a rimmed baking sheet with aluminum foil. Place a wire rack on the prepared sheet. With tongs, place the coated wings on the rack. Place the wings under the broiler for 3 to 5 minutes until they start to brown. Remove from the oven and turn the wings over. Broil the second side for 3 to 5 minutes more until they start to brown. Watch them closely so that they don't burn. Serve with the blue cheese dip.

TIP

If you prefer, take a shortcut with the dip and buy prepared blue cheese salad dressing.

Better-than-Take-Out Sweet-and-Sour Chicken

A perennial favorite. This colorful dish can be on the table in less than 15 minutes.

4 large boneless skinless chicken breasts, cut into 1-inch (2.5 cm) pieces

1 can (8 ounces, or 227 g) pineapple chunks, juice drained and reserved

1 green bell pepper, cut into 1-inch (2.5 cm) chunks

1 red bell pepper, cut into 1-inch (2.5 cm) chunks

2 tablespoons (16 g) cornstarch

2 tablespoons (30 ml) cold water

1 jar (12 fluid ounces, or 355 ml) sweet-and-sour sauce

¼ cup (25 g) sliced scallions, white and green parts

Cooked rice, for serving

—
Serves 6

In the pressure cooking pot, combine the chicken, pineapple juice, and bell peppers. Lock the lid in place. Select High Pressure and 3 minutes cook time.

When the cook time ends, turn off the pressure cooker. Use a quick pressure release. When the valve drops, carefully remove the lid.

In a small bowl, whisk the cornstarch and cold water until smooth. Add the slurry to the pot. Select Simmer/Sauté and simmer, stirring constantly, until the liquid thickens. Stir in the sweet-and-sour sauce and pineapple chunks. Garnish with scallions and serve over rice.

> **TIP**
>
> If needed, add a little water to the pineapple juice to equal ½ cup (120 ml).

Presto Italian Meatball Sandwiches

A tasty meatball sub doesn't have to take all day to make. This shortcut recipe uses frozen ready-to-use meatballs and jarred marinara sauce—it's hot, delicious, and ready in minutes.

1 bag (24 ounces, or 680 g) frozen fully cooked beef Italian meatballs

1 jar (28 fluid ounces, or 828 ml) marinara sauce

4 crusty sub rolls, toasted

2 cups (230 g) shredded mozzarella cheese

—

Serves 4

Add 1 cup (235 ml) water to the pressure cooking pot. Place a steamer basket in the pot and add the frozen meatballs. Lock the lid in place. Select High Pressure and 5 minutes cook time.

When the cook time ends, turn off the pressure cooker. Use a quick pressure release. When the valve drops, carefully remove the lid. Carefully remove the steamer basket and meatballs from the cooking pot. Discard the cooking water. Place the meatballs directly in the cooking pot. Add the marinara and stir to combine. Select Simmer/Sauté and heat until the sauce starts to boil. Switch to the Keep Warm setting until ready to serve.

Pile the meatballs and sauce onto the sub rolls. Top with the mozzarella and place under the preheated broiler to melt the cheese, if desired.

> **TIP**
>
> If you prefer to make your own sauce, you can use a 28-ounce (794 g) can crushed tomatoes in purée, 1½ teaspoons garlic powder, 1 teaspoon dried basil, ¼ teaspoon red pepper flakes, and ¼ teaspoon salt instead, or your favorite recipe.

Chicken Tikka Masala and Rice

If you're an Indian food enthusiast and have a favorite jarred sauce, this recipe will become a favorite in your menu rotation!

½ cup (120 ml) reduced-sodium chicken broth

4 large boneless skinless chicken breasts

1¾ cups (410 ml) water

1½ cups (278 g) long-grain white rice, rinsed

½ teaspoon salt

1 jar (15 fluid ounces, or 444 ml) tikka masala sauce

½ cup (120 ml) heavy cream

Fresh chopped cilantro leaves, for garnish (optional)

—

Serves 4

In the pressure cooking pot, combine the chicken broth and chicken. Put a trivet on the chicken. Place a 7 × 3-inch (18 × 7.5 cm) round cake pan on the trivet and add the water, rice, and salt to it. Lock the lid in place. Select High Pressure and 5 minutes cook time.

When the cook time ends, turn off the pressure cooker. Wait 10 minutes. Use a quick pressure release. When the valve drops, carefully remove the lid. Remove the cake pan and trivet from the cooking pot and fluff the rice with a fork. Cover the rice to keep it warm until ready to serve.

Use a slotted spoon to transfer the chicken from the cooking pot to a cutting board. Cut the chicken into bite-size pieces. Stir the tikka masala sauce into the broth in the pot. Stir in the diced chicken and heavy cream. Serve over rice, if desired, garnished with cilantro.

> **TIP**
>
> Jarred sauces often contain thickeners that can settle to the bottom of the pressure cooking pot and cause problems with the cooker achieving proper pressure. Eliminate this problem by adding jarred sauces after you finish pressure cooking.

Quick-Cooking Chicken and Pierogi Dumplings

Chicken and dumplings is classic comfort food! This shortcut version uses quick-cooking bite-size chicken and frozen, ready-made pierogies instead of traditional dumplings.

1 tablespoon (15 ml) olive oil

1 cup (160 g) diced onion

½ cup (60 g) diced celery

½ cup (65 g) diced carrots

2 cans (14.5 fluid ounces, or 429 ml, each) reduced-sodium chicken broth

4 large boneless skinless chicken breasts, cut into bite-size pieces

1 tablespoon (1 g) dried parsley

1 teaspoon salt

½ teaspoon dried thyme

¼ teaspoon freshly ground black pepper

¼ cup (32 g) cornstarch

¼ cup (60 ml) cold water

⅓ cup (78 ml) half-and-half

12 frozen potato-and-Cheddar pierogies (1 pound, or 454 g, package)

—

Serves 4

Select Browning/Sauté to preheat the pressure cooking pot. When hot, add the olive oil, onion, celery, and carrots. Sauté for 3 minutes, stirring frequently. Stir in the chicken broth, chicken, parsley, salt, thyme, and pepper. Lock the lid in place. Select High Pressure and 3 minutes cook time.

When the cook time ends, turn off the pressure cooker. Use a quick pressure release. When the valve drops, carefully remove the lid.

In a small bowl, whisk the cornstarch and cold water until smooth. Select Simmer/Sauté and add the slurry to the pot, stirring constantly until the sauce comes to a boil and thickens. Stir in the half-and-half. Stir in the pierogies and simmer for 6 minutes, or until they are warmed through.

> **TIP**
>
> Look for potato-and-Cheddar pierogies in the frozen vegetable section of your grocery store.

Easy Pork Chops in Mushroom Gravy

This recipe is adapted from a stovetop recipe my mother-in-law made for my husband growing up. These scrumptious, fall-off-the-bone pork chops in a creamy mushroom gravy have become a favorite on my blog, *Pressure Cooking Today.*

4 bone-in 1-inch-thick (2.5 cm) pork chops

Lemon pepper or your favorite spice blend, for seasoning

2 tablespoons (30 ml) vegetable oil

1½ cups (360 ml) water

1 can (10.5 ounces, or 298 g) condensed cream of mushroom soup

3 tablespoons (45 ml) cold water (optional)

2 tablespoons (14 g) all-purpose flour (optional)

—

Serves 4

Pat the pork chops dry and season liberally with lemon pepper. Select Browning/Sauté and add the vegetable oil to the pressure cooking pot. When the oil begins to sizzle, add 2 chops and brown for about 3 minutes per side. Transfer to a platter and repeat with the remaining 2 chops.

Add the water to deglaze the pot, scraping up any browned bits from the bottom. Stir in the mushroom soup. Add the pork chops and any accumulated juices. Lock the lid in place. Select High Pressure and 18 minutes cook time.

When the cook time ends, turn off the pressure cooker. Let the pressure release naturally for 10 minutes and finish with a quick pressure release. When the valve drops, carefully remove the lid. Transfer the chops to a large serving bowl.

If you prefer a thicker gravy, select Simmer/Sauté and whisk 3 tablespoons (45 ml) cold water with 2 tablespoons (14 g) all-purpose flour until smooth. Add 1 cup (235 ml) gravy to the flour mixture and stir until well combined. Slowly stir this mixture into the gravy in the cooking pot. Pour the gravy over the chops to serve.

TIP

Serve over Creamy Mashed Potatoes (page 79) for an old-fashioned comfort food meal.

CHAPTER 5

30-Minute Meals

When the pressure's on to get dinner on the table in a hurry, turn to these 30-minute meals. All recipes in this section are quick and easy to make. Many are faster and easier than going out—and they're definitely better tasting and better for you.

Chicken Cordon Bleu "Bake"

An easy-to-make, easy-to-serve deconstructed chicken cordon bleu—chicken, ham, and cheese served casserole-style and topped with crunchy bread crumbs.

5 tablespoons (70 g) unsalted butter, plus more for greasing the baking dish

2 large boneless skinless chicken breasts, cut into bite-size pieces

1 cup (235 ml) reduced-sodium chicken broth

1 teaspoon dry mustard

½ teaspoon salt

⅛ teaspoon cayenne pepper

4 medium-size russet potatoes, peeled and cubed

1 cup (50 g) panko bread crumbs

¼ cup (20 g) shredded Parmesan cheese

½ cup (115 g) sour cream

1 cup (110 g) shredded Swiss cheese

8 ounces (227 g) deli ham, diced

—
Serves 6

Grease a 9 × 13-inch (23 × 33 cm) ovenproof dish with butter and set aside.

Select Browning/Sauté and add 2 tablespoons (28 g) butter to the pressure cooking pot to melt. Add the chicken. Sauté for 3 minutes, stirring occasionally. Stir in the chicken broth, dry mustard, salt, and cayenne.

Put a steamer basket in the cooking pot on the chicken. Add the potatoes to the basket. Lock the lid in place. Select High Pressure and 4 minutes cook time. While the chicken cooks, preheat the broiler.

In a small bowl, mix the panko and Parmesan with 3 tablespoons (42 g) melted butter. Set aside.

When the cook time ends, turn off the pressure cooker. Use a quick pressure release. When the valve drops, carefully remove the lid. Remove the steamer basket and potatoes from the pot.

Add the sour cream and Swiss cheese to the cooking pot and stir until the cheese melts. Stir in the potatoes and ham. Pour the mixture into the prepared dish. Top with the panko mixture. Broil for 1 to 2 minutes until golden-brown—watch closely so that it doesn't burn.

> **TIP**
>
> Stir in some thawed frozen peas or vegetables along with the ham to make this a one-pot meal.

Braised Paprika Chicken

This quick weeknight meal combines chicken and a sweet paprika sauce and is served over egg noodles.

2½ pounds (1 kg) boneless skinless chicken thighs

1 tablespoon (8 g) sweet Hungarian paprika, divided

2 tablespoons (30 ml) canola oil

1 tablespoon (14 g) unsalted butter

1 large onion, diced

1 can (14.5 ounces, or 411 g) diced tomatoes, undrained

½ cup (120 ml) reduced-sodium chicken broth

1 teaspoon dried marjoram

1 teaspoon salt

½ teaspoon freshly ground black pepper

⅛ teaspoon red pepper flakes

2 tablespoons (16 g) cornstarch

2 tablespoons (30 ml) cold water

½ cup (115 g) sour cream

Cooked egg noodles, for serving

2 tablespoons (8 g) finely minced fresh parsley leaves, for serving

—

Serves 6

Season the chicken with 1 teaspoon paprika. Select Browning/Sauté to preheat the pressure cooking pot. When hot, add the canola oil and butter. When the butter melts, add 3 chicken thighs and sear briefly. Transfer to a cutting board and add another 3 thighs to the pot. Repeat until all the thighs are browned.

Add the onion to the cooking pot. Sauté for about 3 minutes until tender. Stir in the tomatoes, chicken broth, remaining 2 teaspoons paprika, marjoram, salt, pepper, and red pepper flakes.

Slice the chicken thighs into large bite-size pieces. Add the chicken and any accumulated juices to the pot and stir to combine. Lock the lid in place. Select High Pressure and 4 minutes cook time.

When the cook time ends, turn off the pressure cooker. Use a quick pressure release. When the valve drops, carefully remove the lid.

In a small bowl, whisk the cornstarch and cold water until smooth. Add the slurry to the pot. Select Simmer/Sauté and bring the sauce to a boil, stirring constantly until it thickens. Turn off the pressure cooker and stir in the sour cream. Serve over hot egg noodles and sprinkle with parsley.

> **TIP**
>
> In the United States, most Hungarian paprika has a deep red color and a mild, sweet flavor.

Tamale Pie

This upside-down tamale pie is super easy to make using ingredients you probably have on hand.

1 package (8.5 ounces, or 241 g) corn muffin mix

½ cup (120 ml) milk

1 large egg

1 pound (454 g) lean ground beef

1 tablespoon (15 ml) vegetable oil

½ cup (80 g) finely chopped onion

1 teaspoon garlic powder

1 teaspoon chili powder

1 teaspoon ground cumin

½ teaspoon salt

1 can (14.5 ounces, or 411 g) diced tomatoes, drained

1 can (4.5 ounces, or 128 g) chopped green chilies, drained

1 cup (165 g) frozen corn

1 cup (115 g) shredded Cheddar cheese

—
Serves 6

Spray a 1½-quart (1.4 L) baking dish or a 7-inch (18 cm) round cake pan with nonstick cooking spray. In a large bowl, stir together the muffin mix, milk, and egg until just blended. Spoon the batter into the prepared pan and set aside.

Select Browning/Sauté and when hot, add the ground beef. Cook for about 5 minutes, stirring occasionally, until the meat is crumbled and no longer pink. Transfer to a paper towel–lined plate. Drain any excess fat from the pot.

Add the vegetable oil and onion to the cooking pot. Sauté for about 3 minutes until tender. Add the ground beef, garlic powder, chili powder, cumin, and salt. Sauté for 1 minute more. Turn off the pressure cooker and stir in the tomatoes, green chilies, and corn. Gently spoon the mixture over the cornbread batter.

Wipe out the cooking pot. Pour 1 cup (235 ml) water into the pot and place a trivet in the bottom. Center the pan on a sling and carefully lower the pan onto the trivet. Lock the lid in place. Select High Pressure and 10 minutes cook time.

When the cook time ends, turn off the pressure cooker. Let the pressure release naturally for 5 minutes and finish with a quick pressure release. When the valve drops, carefully remove the lid. Sprinkle the Cheddar on top of the tamale pie. Put the lid back on the pressure cooker until the cheese melts, about 3 minutes. Carefully remove pan from the pressure cooker and serve immediately.

TIP

If you don't have corn muffin mix on hand, make your own: Mix ¾ cup (84 g) all-purpose flour, 1/3 cup (47 g) cornmeal, 2 tablespoons (24 g) sugar, 1 tablespoon (14 g) baking powder, ¼ teaspoon salt, and 2 tablespoons (30 ml) vegetable oil.

Italian Sausage and Spinach Risotto

A creamy, one-pot risotto loaded with sausage, tomatoes, and spinach—but not a drop of cream.

1 pound (454 g) mild Italian sausage, casings removed

1 tablespoon (15 ml) olive oil

½ cup (80 g) finely diced onion

2 cloves garlic, minced

2 cups (384 g) arborio rice

1 can (14.5 ounces, or 411 g) diced tomatoes

5 cups (1.2 L) reduced-sodium chicken broth, divided

1 teaspoon dried basil

⅓ cup (33 g) grated Parmesan cheese, plus more for serving

1 package (6 ounces, or 170 g) fresh baby spinach, coarsely chopped

Salt and freshly ground black pepper, for seasoning

—

Serves 8

Select Browning/Sauté to preheat the pressure cooking pot. When hot, add the sausage. Cook for about 5 minutes, breaking it up as it cooks, until browned and cooked through. Transfer the sausage to a paper towel–lined plate. Drain any excess fat from the pot.

Add the olive oil and onion to the cooking pot. Sauté for about 3 minutes until tender. Add the garlic and sauté for 1 minute more. Stir in the rice and cook for about 2 minutes, stirring frequently, until opaque. Add the sausage. Stir in the tomatoes, 4 cups (946 ml) chicken broth, and the basil. Lock the lid in place. Select High Pressure and 6 minutes cook time.

When the cook time ends, turn off the pressure cooker. Use a quick pressure release. When the valve drops, carefully remove the lid. Select Simmer/Sauté and stir in the remaining 1 cup (235 ml) chicken broth. Check the rice for doneness; if needed, continue simmering and stirring until tender. Stir in the Parmesan and spinach. Cook for about 1 minute until wilted. Season with salt and pepper to taste. Serve topped with more Parmesan.

> **TIP**
>
> Arborio rice is an Italian short-grain rice with a higher starch content, making it creamy as it cooks.

Game Day Potatoes

These potatoes are perfect to serve for the big game—or any day you're craving something cheesy and delicious.

1 pound (454 g) extra-lean ground beef

2 teaspoons chili powder

1 teaspoon onion powder

½ teaspoon garlic powder

½ teaspoon ground cumin

¼ teaspoon salt

Dash cayenne pepper

6 medium-size russet potatoes, cut into wedges

3 cups (340 g) shredded Cheddar cheese

Sour cream, scallions, olives, and hot sauce, for topping

—
Serves 6

Select Browning/Sauté to preheat the pressure cooking pot. When hot, add the ground beef. Cook for about 5 minutes, stirring occasionally, until the meat is crumbled and no longer pink. Add the chili powder, onion powder, garlic powder, cumin, salt, and cayenne. Cook for 1 minute more. Transfer the beef to a bowl.

Wipe out the pressure cooking pot. Pour 1 cup (235 ml) water into the pot and place a steamer basket in it. Add the potato wedges. Lock the lid in place. Select High Pressure and 5 minutes cook time.

When the cook time ends, turn off the pressure cooker. Use a quick pressure release. When the valve drops, carefully remove the lid. Check the potatoes to make sure they're tender; if they need more time, put the lid back on and let them steam for 1 to 2 minutes more.

Preheat the broiler.

Spread the potatoes into a single layer on an aluminum foil-lined baking sheet. Sprinkle the seasoned ground beef evenly on top. Sprinkle the Cheddar evenly on top of the meat. Broil until the cheese melts and starts to brown. Serve topped with sour cream, scallions, olives, and hot sauce, if desired.

> **TIP**
>
> The potatoes cook best when they're in cut into uniform sizes. I first halve the potato lengthwise and cut each half into thirds lengthwise—similar in shape to large steak fries.

Cashew Chicken

My boys are crazy about cashews, so they love the crunchy cashews mixed with the juicy chicken in a sweet, not-too-spicy sauce.

1½ pounds (680 g) boneless skinless chicken breasts, diced into bite-size peices

Freshly ground black pepper, for seasoning

1 tablespoon (15 ml) vegetable oil

¼ cup (60 ml) reduced-sodium chicken broth

¼ cup (60 ml) low-sodium soy sauce

3 tablespoons (60 g) honey

2 tablespoons (30 ml) rice vinegar

½ teaspoon chili-garlic sauce

2 tablespoons (16 g) cornstarch

2 tablespoons (30 ml) cold water

½ cup (68 g) roasted cashew halves

Prepared rice, for serving

4 scallions, white and green parts, sliced, for serving

—
Serves 6

Lightly season the chicken with pepper. Select Browning/Sauté to preheat the pressure cooking pot. When hot, add the vegetable oil and chicken. Sauté for about 3 minutes. Stir in the chicken broth, soy sauce, honey, rice vinegar, and chili-garlic sauce. Lock the lid in place. Select High Pressure and 3 minutes cook time.

When the cook time ends, turn off the pressure cooker. Use a quick pressure release. When the valve drops, carefully remove the lid.

In a small bowl, whisk the cornstarch and cold water until smooth. Gradually add the slurry to the pot. Select Simmer/Sauté and simmer, stirring constantly, until the sauce thickens. Stir in the cashews and simmer for 2 minutes more. Serve over rice, if desired, and garnish with scallions.

TIP

I like to use cashew halves in this recipe so that you get a cashew in every bite. If you have whole cashews, break them in half.

Kung Pao Chicken

A slightly spicy Kung Pao Chicken with colorful vegetables, red pepper flakes, and crunchy peanuts. Substitute whole dried chilies for the red pepper flakes for an extra pop of color and heat.

1 tablespoon (15 ml) sesame oil

3 large cloves garlic, minced

2 teaspoons grated peeled fresh ginger

½ teaspoon red pepper flakes

⅓ cup (78 ml) low-sodium soy sauce

½ cup (120 ml) reduced-sodium chicken broth

2 tablespoons (30 ml) seasoned rice vinegar

2 teaspoons sugar

3 boneless skinless chicken breasts (about 1½ pound, or 680 g), diced into bite-size pieces

3 tablespoons (24 g) cornstarch

3 tablespoons (45 ml) cold water

1 cup (130 g) sliced carrots

1½ cups (93 g) snow peas

6 scallions, white and green parts, chopped

½ cup (75 g) roasted peanuts, chopped

Cooked rice or noodles, for serving

—
Serves 6

Select Browning/Sauté and add the sesame oil, garlic, ginger, and red pepper flakes to the pressure cooking pot. Stir-fry for 30 seconds, stirring constantly. Stir in the soy sauce, chicken broth, rice vinegar, and sugar. Add the chicken and stir to combine. Lock the lid in place. Select High Pressure and 3 minutes cook time.

When the cook time ends, turn off the pressure cooker. Use a quick pressure release. When the valve drops, carefully remove the lid.

In a small bowl, whisk the cornstarch and cold water until smooth. Add the slurry to the pot. Select Simmer/Sauté and simmer, stirring constantly, until the sauce thickens. Stir in the carrots and snow peas and simmer for about 5 minutes until tender. Stir in the scallions, leaving a few for garnishing, and the peanuts. Serve over rice or noodles, if desired, and top with the remaining scallions.

TIP

I keep a container of dry-roasted salted peanuts in the pantry for snacks and use those in this recipe; if you prefer, use unsalted peanuts.

Tuscan Garlic Chicken Fettuccine

You'll enjoy this tempting chicken dish in a rich, colorful, creamy garlic-Parmesan sauce served over fettuccine.

3 large boneless skinless chicken breasts (about 1½ pounds, or 680 g), cut into bite-size pieces

Salt and freshly ground black pepper, for seasoning

2 tablespoons (30 ml) olive oil

1 tablespoon (10 g) minced or pressed garlic (about 8 cloves)

1½ cups (360 ml) reduced-sodium chicken broth

½ teaspoon dried basil

½ teaspoon Italian seasoning

⅛ teaspoon red pepper flakes

2 tablespoons (16 g) cornstarch

2 tablespoons (30 ml) cold water

1 cup (100 g) grated Parmesan cheese

½ cup (120 ml) heavy cream

2 cups (60 g) fresh spinach

¼ cup (14 g) sun-dried tomatoes packed in oil, chopped

1 pound (454 g) fettuccine, prepared according to package directions

—
Serves 6

Select Browning/Sauté to preheat the pressure cooking pot. Generously season the chicken with salt and pepper. Add the olive oil and chicken to the cooking pot. Sauté for 3 minutes, stirring occasionally. Add the garlic and sauté for 30 seconds more. Stir in the chicken broth, basil, Italian seasoning, and red pepper flakes. Lock the lid in place. Select High Pressure and 3 minutes cook time.

When the cook time ends, turn off the pressure cooker. Use a quick pressure release. When the valve drops, carefully remove the lid.

In a small bowl, whisk the cornstarch and cold water until smooth. Add the slurry to the pot. Select Simmer/Sauté and bring the sauce to a boil, stirring constantly until it thickens. Turn off the pressure cooker. Stir in the Parmesan until melted. Stir in the heavy cream, spinach, and sun-dried tomatoes.

Add the fettuccine to the cooking pot and toss to combine. Serve immediately.

> **TIP**
>
> I use sundried tomatoes in oil for this recipe. You could use dry-packed sundried tomatoes if you prefer. Hydrate in a little warm water to plump them before chopping.

Chicken Fettuccine Alfredo

When we go out to an Italian restaurant, my boys always order Chicken Fettuccine Alfredo. With this pressure cooker version, I can make it at home for a fraction of the cost of eating out.

2 large boneless skinless chicken breasts (about 1 pound, or 454 g)

1 teaspoon salt, plus more for seasoning

Freshly ground black pepper, for seasoning

¼ cup (56 g) unsalted butter

3 cloves garlic, minced

4 cups (955 ml) water, divided

1 pound (454 g) fettuccine

1 cup (100 g) grated Parmesan cheese, plus more for serving

1 cup (235 ml) heavy cream

¼ cup (15 g) chopped fresh flat-leaf parsley leaves (optional)

3 tablespoons (24 g) cornstarch

3 tablespoons (45 ml) cold water

—

Serves 6

Generously season the chicken with salt and pepper. Select Browning/Sauté to preheat the pressure cooking pot. When hot, add the butter to melt. Add the chicken. Cook for about 3 minutes per side until browned. Transfer the chicken to a plate.

Add the garlic to the pot and sauté for 1 minute. Add 1 cup (235 ml) water to deglaze the pot, scraping up any browned bits from the bottom. Stir in the salt. Add the chicken to the pot. Place the fettuccine on the chicken and add enough of the remaining 3 cups (720 ml) water to just cover the pasta. Lock the lid in place. Select High Pressure and 5 minutes cook time.

When the cook time ends, turn off the pressure cooker. Use a quick pressure release. When the valve drops, carefully remove the lid. Transfer the chicken to a cutting board and cut it into strips. Stir the pasta. If needed, select Simmer/Sauté and continue to cook, stirring often, until the fettuccine is tender. Stir in the Parmesan a little at a time until melted. Stir in the heavy cream and parsley.

In a small bowl, whisk the cornstarch and cold water until smooth. Select Simmer/Sauté and add the slurry to the pot, stirring constantly until the sauce thickens. Stir in the sliced chicken and season with additional salt and pepper to taste.

TIP

When browning meat, it's important to pat the meat dry with paper towels so the meat browns and doesn't steam.

Spaghetti Squash Matrichana

The pressure cooker is the best way to cook spaghetti squash. This matrichana sauce recipe was given to me by my Spanish teacher—it's a flavorful sauce made with tomatoes simmered with onion, garlic, and bacon, and spiced with plenty of black pepper.

8 slices peppered bacon, diced

1 large onion, diced

1 tablespoon (10 g) minced garlic

2 cans (28 ounces, or 794 g, each) diced tomatoes, undrained

½ cup (120 ml) water

1 teaspoon salt, plus more as needed

¼ teaspoon freshly ground black pepper, plus more as needed

1 medium spaghetti squash (about 3 pounds, or 1.4 g), stem end removed, halved lengthwise then crosswise into 4 pieces, seeds and pulp removed

—

Serves 6

Select Browning/Sauté and add the bacon to the pressure cooking pot. Fry for about 5 minutes until crisp, stirring frequently. Transfer the bacon to a paper towel–lined plate, leaving the bacon fat in the pot.

Add the onion. Sauté for about 3 minutes, stirring frequently, until the onion softens and begins to brown. Add the garlic and sauté for 1 minute more. Stir in the tomatoes, water, salt, and pepper. Place the squash pieces in the cooking pot with the sauce. Lock the lid in place. Select High Pressure and 7 minutes cook time.

When the cook time ends, turn off the pressure cooker. Use a quick pressure release. When the valve drops, carefully remove the lid. Use tongs and a large fork to carefully remove the squash from the cooking pot.

Select Simmer/Sauté and simmer the sauce to thicken. Stir in the bacon. Season with salt and pepper to taste.

When the squash is cool enough to handle, use a fork to scrape the flesh into strands. Serve topped with the sauce.

> **TIP**
>
> You can use regular bacon in this recipe, but you'll need to double the amount of pepper.

Sweet Teriyaki Pork Tenderloin

Pork tenderloin is a long, thin strip of pork that's very tender and cooks quickly in the pressure cooker. I've paired it with a flavorful sweet teriyaki sauce that's perfect served over rice.

1¼ pounds (567 g) pork tenderloin

Salt and freshly ground black pepper, for seasoning

1 tablespoon (15 ml) vegetable oil

½ cup (120 ml) reduced-sodium chicken broth

½ cup (120 ml) teriyaki sauce

¼ cup (60 g) packed light brown sugar

2 tablespoons (30 ml) white vinegar

Pinch red pepper flakes

2 tablespoons (16 g) cornstarch

2 tablespoons (30 ml) cold water

Cooked white rice, chopped scallions, toasted sesame seeds, for serving

—

Serves 4

Generously season the tenderloin with salt and pepper. Select Browning/Sauté and add the vegetable oil to the cooking pot. When the oil is hot, add the tenderloin and brown for about 3 minutes per side. Transfer to a platter.

Stir in the chicken broth to deglaze the pot, scraping up any browned bits from the bottom. Add the teriyaki sauce, brown sugar, white vinegar, and red pepper. Stir to combine.

Slice the tenderloin into 2-inch -thick (5 cm) medallions. Add the medallions and any accumulated juices to the pot. Lock the lid in place. Select High Pressure and 1 minute cook time.

When the cook time ends, turn off the pressure cooker. Let the pressure release naturally for 10 minutes and finish with a quick pressure release. When the valve drops, carefully remove the lid.

In a small bowl, whisk the cornstarch and cold water until smooth. Add the slurry to the pot. Select Simmer/Sauté and bring the sauce to a boil, stirring constantly until it thickens. Serve over white rice, if desired, garnished with scallions and sesame seeds.

TIP

Pork tenderloin is generally sold with two tenderloins in a package. If you prefer, cook both at the same time without changing the cook time or sauce ingredients.

Korean Beef Rice Bowl

Turn inexpensive ground beef into a flavorful Asian-inspired meal.

2 tablespoons (30 ml) vegetable oil, divided

1 pound (454 g) ground beef

1 cup (160 g) diced onion

3 cloves garlic, minced

¼ cup (60 ml) low-sodium soy sauce

¼ cup (60 ml) reduced-sodium beef broth

⅓ cup (75 g) packed light brown sugar

2 teaspoons sesame oil

¼ teaspoon red pepper flakes

¼ teaspoon ground ginger

1¾ cups (410 ml) water

1½ cups (278 g) long-grain white rice, rinsed

½ teaspoon salt

2 tablespoons (16 g) cornstarch

2 tablespoons (30 ml) cold water

3 scallions, white and green parts, sliced

—

Serves 4 to 6

Select Browning/Sauté to preheat the pressure cooking pot. When hot, add 1 tablespoon (15 ml) vegetable oil and the ground beef. Cook for about 5 minutes, stirring frequently, until the beef is browned and crumbled. Transfer to a paper towel–lined plate. Drain any excess fat from the pot.

Add the remaining 1 tablespoon (15 ml) vegetable oil and the onion to the cooking pot. Sauté for about 3 minutes, stirring occasionally, until tender. Add the garlic and cook for 1 minute more. Stir in the soy sauce, beef broth, brown sugar, sesame oil, red pepper flakes, and ginger. Stir in the browned beef.

Place a trivet on the beef in the cooking pot. Place a 7 × 3-inch (18 × 7.5 cm) round cake pan or other flat-bottomed dish on the trivet and add the water, rice, and salt. Lock the lid in place. Select High Pressure and 5 minutes cook time.

When the cook time ends, turn off the pressure cooker. Let the pressure release naturally for 10 minutes and finish with a quick pressure release. When the valve drops, carefully remove the lid. Remove the cake pan and trivet from the cooking pot. Fluff the rice with a fork and cover it to keep warm until ready to serve.

In a small bowl, whisk the cornstarch and 2 tablespoons (30 ml) cold water until smooth. Add the slurry to the pot. Select Simmer/Sauté and bring the sauce to a boil, stirring constantly until it thickens. Serve the beef over the rice garnished with scallions.

TIP

Serve drizzled with Go Chu Jang Korean Chili Sauce or Sriracha if you like a little more heat.

CHAPTER 6

Sunday Suppers

On Sunday, my mom always cooked a hot, homemade meal. While she reserved these wonderful meals for Sunday, making them in a pressure cooker allows you to enjoy them any night of the week that you have a little extra time.

Beef Stroganoff

My family loves this braised beef with golden mushrooms and flavorful, creamy gravy, served over egg noodles.

2 pounds (907 g) beef round steak, cut into 1-inch (2.5 cm) pieces

Salt and freshly ground black pepper, for seasoning

2 tablespoons (30 ml) vegetable oil, divided, plus more as needed

1 medium-size onion, chopped

2 cloves garlic, minced or pressed

2 tablespoons (32 g) tomato paste

1½ cups (360 ml) reduced-sodium beef broth

1 tablespoon (14 g) unsalted butter

1 package (12 ounces, or 340 g) white mushrooms, sliced

2 tablespoons (16 g) cornstarch

3 tablespoons (45 ml) cold water

⅓ cup (77 g) sour cream

Cooked egg noodles, for serving

—
Serves 6

Season the beef generously with salt and pepper. Select Browning/Sauté to preheat the pressure cooking pot. When hot, add 1 tablespoon (15 ml) vegetable oil. Brown the meat in batches, about 3 minutes per batch, until all the meat is browned. Add more oil as needed. Do not crowd the pot. Transfer the browned meat to a plate.

Add the onion to the cooking pot. Sauté for about 3 minutes, stirring frequently, until soft and beginning to brown. Add the garlic and tomato paste. Sauté for 1 minute. Stir in the beef broth to deglaze the pot, scraping up any brown bits from the bottom. Add the browned beef and any accumulated juices. Lock the lid in place. Select High Pressure and 18 minutes cook time.

While the beef cooks, heat a large skillet or sauté pan over medium-high heat until hot. Add the remaining 1 tablespoon (15 ml) vegetable oil and butter. When the butter melts, add the mushrooms. Cook for about 5 minutes until golden. When the cook time ends, turn off the pressure cooker. Let the pressure release naturally for 10 minutes and finish with a quick pressure release. When the valve drops, carefully remove the lid.

In a small bowl, whisk the cornstarch and cold water until smooth. Add the slurry to the pot. Select Simmer/Sauté and bring the gravy to a boil, stirring constantly until it thickens. In a separate bowl, combine ⅓ cup (78.3 ml) gravy with the sour cream and mix well. Add the sour cream mixture to the cooking pot and stir until well blended. Serve over egg noodles.

Fork-Tender Beef Brisket

My sister made beef brisket for a family party, and it was so tender and flavorful I asked her for the recipe so I could adapt for the pressure cooker. This brisket marinates overnight but has only 1 hour cook time in the pressure cooker, compared to the usual 6 to 8 hours in the oven.

¼ teaspoon celery salt

¼ teaspoon seasoned salt

¼ teaspoon garlic salt

3 pounds (1.4 kg) beef brisket, fat trimmed to ¼ inch (0.6 cm)

2 tablespoons (30 ml) liquid smoke

1 tablespoon (15 ml) Worcestershire sauce

1 cup (250 g) barbecue sauce, plus more for serving

½ cup (120 ml) water

—

Serves 6

In a small bowl, combine the celery salt, seasoned salt, and garlic salt. Rub the spices into the brisket and place it in a large, heavy-duty zipper bag. Add the liquid smoke and Worcestershire sauce. Seal the bag and refrigerate to marinate overnight.

In the pressure cooking pot, stir together the barbecue sauce and water. Add the brisket and any accumulated juices. Lock the lid in place. Select High Pressure and 55 minutes cook time.

When the cook time ends, turn off the pressure cooker. Let the pressure release naturally for 15 minutes and finish with a quick pressure release. When the valve drops, carefully remove the lid. Carefully transfer the brisket to a large platter and slice the meat across the grain.

In a small bowl, stir together a little cooking liquid with some additional barbecue sauce and drizzle it over the meat just before serving.

> **TIP**
>
> You may have to cut the brisket in half to fit it in the cooking pot. If this happens, try to fit the pieces side by side rather than stacking one on top of the other. If serving a crowd, shred the brisket and serve it on rolls, pulled-pork style.

Corned Beef and Cabbage

Everybody's Irish on St. Patrick's Day. Celebrate with a good old-fashioned Irish meal—cooked faster in the pressure cooker.

3 pounds (1.4 kg) flat-cut corned beef brisket with seasoning packet

1 quart (946 ml) reduced-sodium beef broth

1 large onion, quartered

8 cloves garlic

18 small red potatoes

6 large carrots, each cut into 3 pieces

1 small head cabbage, cut into 6 wedges

—

Serves 6

Rinse the corned beef under cold water to remove excess salt and gel. In the pressure cooking pot, combine the seasoning packet, beef broth, onion, and garlic. Put a rack in the cooking pot and place the corned beef on the rack. Lock the lid in place. Select High Pressure and 90 minutes cook time.

When the cook time ends, turn off the pressure cooker. Let the pressure release naturally for 10 minutes and finish with a quick pressure release. When the valve drops, carefully remove the lid. Transfer the corned beef to a serving plate and cover with aluminum foil until ready to serve.

Remove the rack from the pressure cooking pot. Add the potatoes, carrots, and cabbage to the liquid in the pot. Lock the lid in place. Select High Pressure and 3 minutes cook time.

When the cook time ends, turn off the pressure cooker. Use a quick pressure release. When the valve drops, carefully remove the lid. Check the potatoes to see if they're tender; if needed, select Simmer/Sauté and cook until they reach your desired tenderness. Serve immediately.

TIP

Corned beef is a salt-cured beef brisket. It's called "corned" because the brisket is preserved in large-grain rock salt, which is known as salt corns. Don't skip rinsing the corned beef under cold water or your finished dish will be very salty.

Salisbury Steak with Mushroom Gravy

Despite its name, Salisbury steak is actually made with hamburger mixed with other ingredients, shaped like a steak, and served with a flavorful mushroom gravy.

1 pound (454 g) lean ground beef

⅓ cup (38 g) dried bread crumbs

1 egg, beaten

1 teaspoon onion powder

1 teaspoon garlic powder

1 teaspoon salt, plus more as needed

½ teaspoon freshly ground black pepper, plus more as needed

½ teaspoon Worcestershire sauce

2 tablespoons (30 ml) vegetable oil, plus more as needed

½ cup (80 g) chopped onion

1 cup (70 g) sliced mushrooms

1 can (14.5 fluid ounces, or 429 ml) reduced-sodium beef broth

3 tablespoons (21 g) all-purpose flour

¼ cup (60 ml) water

Creamy Mashed Potatoes (page 79), for serving

—
Serves 4

In a large bowl, mix the ground beef, bread crumbs, egg, onion powder, garlic powder, salt, pepper and Worcestershire sauce until just combined. Shape the mixture into 4 patties, each about 1 inch (2.5 cm) thick.

Select Browning/Sauté to preheat the pressure cooking pot. When hot, add the vegetable oil. Brown the patties, 2 at a time, for about 3 minutes per side. Transfer to a plate.

If needed, add more oil to the pot along with the onion. Sauté for about 3 minutes until tender. Add the mushrooms and sauté for 2 minutes more. Stir in the beef broth to deglaze the pot, scraping up any browned bits from the bottom. Add the browned patties to the pot. Lock the lid in place. Select High Pressure and 2 minutes cook time.

When the cook time ends, turn off the pressure cooker. Use a quick pressure release. When the valve drops, carefully remove the lid.

In a small bowl, whisk the flour and water until smooth. Move the patties to one side of the pot. Gradually whisk the slurry into the pot. Select Simmer/Sauté and bring the sauce to a boil, stirring constantly until it thickens. Season with salt and pepper to taste. Serve over Creamy Mashed Potatoes (page 79), if desired.

TIP

Remove the patties from the cooking pot before adding the flour slurry if you prefer.

Beef Bourguignon

This classic French stew is one of my favorite meals—chunks of beef paired with smoky bacon and simmered in a burgundy sauce until tender.

6 slices bacon, chopped into ½-inch (1 cm) pieces

3 pounds (1.4 kg) stew beef, cut into 2-inch (5 cm) cubes

1 teaspoon salt, plus more for seasoning

½ teaspoon freshly ground black pepper, plus more for seasoning

2 cloves garlic, finely chopped or pressed

1½ cups (355 ml) red wine

¾ cup (175 ml) reduced-sodium beef broth

1 tablespoon (16 g) tomato paste

½ teaspoon dried thyme

1 bay leaf

1 tablespoon (15 ml) vegetable oil

1 tablespoon (14 g) unsalted butter

1 package (8 ounces, or 227 g) mushrooms, sliced

2 large carrots, sliced diagonally into ½-inch (1 cm) slices

20 frozen pearl onions

¼ cup (28 g) all-purpose flour

¼ cup (60 ml) cold water

Cooked noodles or Creamy Mashed Potatoes (page 79), for serving

2 tablespoons (8 g) chopped fresh parsley leaves

—
Serves 6

Select Browning/Sauté and add the bacon to the pressure cooking pot. Fry for about 5 minutes until crisp, stirring frequently. Transfer the bacon to a paper towel–lined plate, leaving the bacon fat in the pot.

Season the beef with salt and pepper. Add it to the pot in batches and brown in the bacon fat for about 5 minutes on one side. Transfer the browned beef to a platter. Add the garlic and sauté for 30 seconds, stirring constantly. Add the red wine to deglaze the pot, scraping up any browned bits from the bottom. Let the wine cook until reduced to about 1 cup (240 ml). Stir in the beef broth, tomato paste, thyme, bay leaf, salt, and pepper. Add the browned beef along with any accumulated juices. Lock the lid in place. Select High Pressure and 20 minutes cook time. While the beef cooks, heat a large skillet or sauté pan over medium-high heat until hot. Add the vegetable oil and butter. When the butter melts, add the mushrooms and cook for about 5 minutes until golden. Season with salt and pepper to taste. Set aside.

When the cook time ends, turn off the pressure cooker. Let the pressure release naturally for 10 minutes and finish with a quick pressure release. When the valve drops, carefully remove the lid. Add the carrots and onions to the pot. Lock the lid in place. Select High Pressure and 5 minutes cook time.

TIP

Use a dry red wine, such as a Burgundy, Pinot Noir, or Cabernet Sauvignon.

When the cook time ends, turn off the pressure cooker. Let the pressure release naturally for 10 minutes and finish with a quick pressure release. When the valve drops, carefully remove the lid.

In a small bowl, whisk the flour and water until smooth. Add about ½ cup (120 ml) hot broth to the flour mixture and stir to combine. Add the slurry to the pot. Select Simmer/Sauté and bring the sauce to a boil, stirring constantly until it thickens. Add the mushrooms and bacon and stir to coat with the sauce. Serve over noodles or Creamy Mashed Potatoes (page 79), if desired, garnished with parsley.

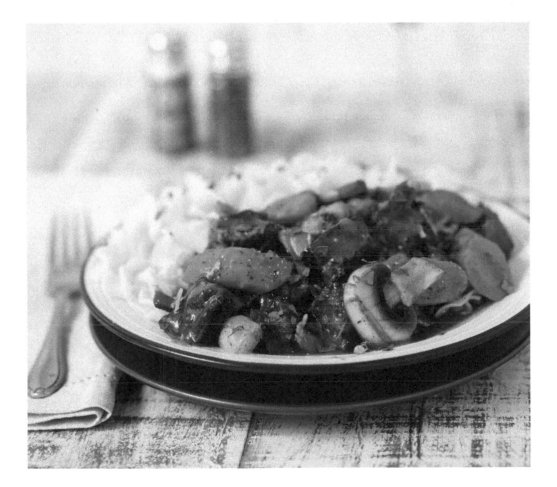

Pepper-Crusted Steak with Parmesan-Garlic Butter

Nothing beats a great steak on the grill—but if grilling is not an option, here's how to get great flavor in a pressure cooker.

¼ cup (56 g) unsalted butter, at room temperature

1 tablespoon (6 g) finely grated Parmesan cheese

¼ teaspoon garlic salt

4 (6 ounces, or 170 g, each) top sirloin steaks (about 1½ inches, or 3.5 cm, thick)

Salt and freshly ground black pepper, for seasoning

1 tablespoon (15 ml) olive oil

—

Serves 4

In a small bowl, blend the butter, Parmesan, and garlic salt. Set aside.

Pat the steaks dry and season with salt and a generous amount of pepper. Press the seasonings firmly to adhere to the meat.

Add 1 cup (235 ml) water to the pressure cooking pot and place a trivet in the bottom. Place the steaks on the trivet. Lock the lid in place. Select High Pressure and 1 minute cook time for a steak that's medium to medium-well. (Adjust the cook time if your steaks are thicker or thinner or to achieve your desired doneness.)

When the cook time ends, turn off the pressure cooker. Let the pressure release naturally for 10 minutes. With 5 minutes left in the natural pressure release, preheat a cast iron or heavy-bottomed skillet over medium-high heat. After 10 minutes, use a quick pressure release. When the valve drops, carefully remove the lid.

Add the olive oil to the preheated skillet. Transfer the steaks to the hot skillet. Cook for about 1 minute until a dark crust forms. Flip and cook for 1 minute more. Remove the skillet from the heat and top each steak with 1 tablespoon (14 g) compound butter. Serve immediately.

> **TIP**
>
> If the steaks won't fit side by side on the rack, stack 2 crosswise on top of each other.

Melt-in-Your-Mouth Baby Back Ribs

When you cook ribs in the pressure cooker before grilling them, you get the best of both worlds—moist fall-off-the-bone meat from the pressure cooker and caramelized, finger-licking-good coating from the grill.

2 tablespoons (30 g) packed light brown sugar

1 tablespoon (8 g) chili powder

1 tablespoon (18 g) salt

1 teaspoon freshly ground black pepper

1 teaspoon garlic powder

1 teaspoon onion powder

1 rack pork baby back ribs

1 cup (250 g) barbecue sauce

—
Serves 4

In a small bowl, combine the brown sugar, chili powder, salt, pepper, garlic powder, and onion powder. Set aside.

Pat the ribs dry with paper towels and place them on a work surface. Peel the membrane off the back of the ribs. Cut the rack into sections to fit inside the pressure cooking pot. Liberally season the ribs on both sides with the spice mixture, rubbing it into the ribs.

Add 1 cup (235 ml) water and a rack to the pressure cooking pot. Place the ribs on the rack, so the bones are facing up. Lock the lid in place. Select High Pressure and 18 minutes cook time.

When the cook time ends, turn off the pressure cooker. Let the pressure release naturally for 10 minutes and finish with a quick pressure release. When the valve drops, carefully remove the lid.

Preheat a grill to medium-high heat. Coat one side of the ribs with barbecue sauce. Place them on the grill, sauce-side down, and grill for 3 minutes. Coat the other side with sauce, flip, and grill for 3 minutes more. Slather on additional barbecue sauce and grill each side for 3 minutes more. Alternatively, finish the ribs under the preheated broiler following the same sequence. Serve immediately.

TIP

The ribs can be made ahead and reheated on the grill. After pressure cooking, cool to room temperature and refrigerate until ready to grill.

Chicken Marsala

Chicken Marsala is a classic dish made with chicken, mushrooms, and Marsala wine. This version includes bacon, which gives the dish a smoky taste that complements the richness of the wine.

4 slices peppered bacon, diced

3 pounds (1.4 kg) boneless skinless chicken thighs, trimmed

Salt and freshly ground black pepper, for seasoning

½ cup (120 ml) sweet Marsala wine

1 cup (235 ml) reduced-sodium chicken broth

1 tablespoon (15 ml) vegetable oil

3 tablespoons (42 g) unsalted butter, divided

1 package (8 ounces, or 227 g) mushrooms, sliced

2 tablespoons (16 g) cornstarch

3 tablespoons (45 ml) cold water

2 tablespoons (8 g) chopped fresh parsley leaves

—

Serves 6

TIP

When I make chicken in the pressure cooker, I prefer chicken thighs. The pressure breaks down the fat and tissue, which leaves the meat much more tender and moist than chicken breasts. However, substitute chicken breasts in this recipe, if you prefer.

Select Browning/Sauté and add the bacon to the pressure cooking pot. Fry for about 5 minutes until crisp, stirring frequently. Transfer the bacon to a paper towel–lined plate, leaving the bacon fat in the pot.

Season the chicken with salt and pepper. Add it to the pot in batches and brown for about 3 minutes per side in the bacon fat. Transfer the browned chicken to a platter.

Add the Marsala wine to deglaze the pot, scraping up any browned bits from the bottom. Let the liquid almost completely evaporate to concentrate the flavor. Stir in the chicken broth and return the browned chicken to the pot along with any accumulated juices. Lock the lid in place. Select High Pressure and 10 minutes cook time. When the cook time ends, use a quick pressure release. When the valve drops, carefully remove the lid. Transfer the chicken to a serving dish.

Heat a large skillet or sauté pan over medium-high heat until hot. Add the vegetable oil and 1 tablespoon (14 g) butter. When the butter melts, add the mushrooms and cook for about 5 minutes until golden. Season with salt and pepper.

In a small bowl, whisk the cornstarch and cold water until smooth. Add the slurry to the pot. Select Simmer/Sauté and bring the sauce to a boil, stirring constantly. Stir in the remaining 2 tablespoons (28 g) butter. Add the mushrooms and stir to coat with the sauce. Season with salt and pepper to taste, then combine with the chicken in the serving bowl. Serve topped with crumbled bacon and parsley.

Chicken Cacciatore

Cacciatore is Italian for "hunter," so this chicken is prepared hunter style with onions, tomatoes, bell peppers, and herbs.

4 large bone-in skinless chicken breasts (about 2 pounds, or 907 g)

½ teaspoon salt, plus more for seasoning

¼ teaspoon freshly ground black pepper, plus more for seasoning

3 tablespoons (45 ml) vegetable oil, divided

1 green bell pepper, chopped

1 large onion, chopped

2 cloves garlic, minced or pressed

1 can (14.5 ounces, or 411 g) diced tomatoes, undrained

1 jar (4.5 ounces, or 127.5 g) sliced mushrooms, drained

½ teaspoon dried oregano

½ teaspoon dried basil

Freshly grated Parmesan cheese, for serving

Fresh parsley leaves, for serving

—

Serves 4

Generously season the chicken with salt and pepper. Select Browning/Sauté to preheat the pressure cooking pot. When hot, add 1 tablespoon (15 ml) vegetable oil. Brown the chicken in 2 batches for about 3 minutes per side. Do not crowd the pot. Transfer the browned chicken to a platter.

Add the remaining 2 tablespoons (30 ml) vegetable oil to the pot. Add the green bell pepper, onion, and garlic. Sauté for about 3 minutes, stirring occasionally, until tender. Stir in the tomatoes, mushrooms, oregano, basil, salt, and pepper. Add the chicken and any accumulated juices. Lock the lid in place. Select High Pressure and 6 minutes cook time.

When the cook time ends, turn off the pressure cooker. Let the pressure cooker stand naturally for 5 minutes, then finish with a quick pressure release. When the valve drops, carefully remove the lid. Using tongs, transfer the chicken to a platter and cover with aluminum foil to keep warm. Select Simmer/Sauté and boil the sauce until it thickens. Spoon the sauce over the chicken and sprinkle with Parmesan and parsley to serve.

TIP

If you have fresh basil, you can substitute 2 teaspoons finely chopped fresh basil for the dried basil.

Turkey Breast with Turkey Gravy

Turkey breast cooked in the pressure cooker is super moist and juicy, and cooking a turkey this way saves you lots of flavorful liquid to make a wonderful turkey gravy.

6½ pounds (3 kg) bone-in skin-on turkey breast

Salt and freshly ground black pepper, for seasoning

1 can (14.5 fluid ounces, or 429 ml) reduced-sodium turkey broth or chicken broth

1 large onion, quartered

1 rib celery, cut into large pieces

1 sprig fresh thyme

3 tablespoons (24 g) cornstarch

3 tablespoons (45 ml) cold water

—

Serves 8

Season the turkey breast liberally with salt and pepper. Put a trivet in the bottom of the pressure cooking pot. Add the turkey broth, onion, celery, and thyme. Place the turkey in the pot, breast-side up. Lock the lid in place. Select High Pressure and 30 minutes cook time.

When the cook time ends, turn off the pressure cooker. Let the pressure release naturally for 10 minutes and finish with a quick pressure release. When the valve drops, carefully remove the lid. Use an instant-read thermometer to check the turkey. It should be 165°F (74°C) in the thickest part of the breast. If needed, relock the lid and cook at High Pressure for a few more minutes.

Carefully transfer the turkey to a large plate. Cover with aluminum foil. Strain the broth and skim off the fat. Return it to the pot.

In a small bowl, whisk the cornstarch and cold water until smooth. Add the slurry to the pot. Select Simmer/Sauté and bring the broth to a boil, stirring constantly until it thickens. Season with salt and pepper to taste.

Remove and discard the skin. Slice the turkey and serve immediately with the gravy.

TIP

My family doesn't care for the skin; if your family does, place the turkey on a broiling pan after pressure cooking and pop it in a 450°F (230°C or gas mark 8) oven for 5 to 10 minutes to crisp the skin.

Eggplant Lasagna Rolls

A cross between eggplant Parmesan and lasagna, these Eggplant Lasagna Rolls are easy to make and easy to serve.

1 large eggplant, ends removed, peeled, and sliced lengthwise into ¼-inch (0.6 cm) slices

½ teaspoon salt, plus more for salting the eggplant

1 cup (250 g) whole-milk ricotta cheese

⅓ cup (33 g) grated Parmesan cheese

1 large egg

2 tablespoons (8 g) chopped fresh parsley leaves

½ teaspoon garlic powder

¼ teaspoon ground black pepper

1 cup (240 ml) marinara sauce (store-bought or homemade), divided

1 tablespoon (15 ml) vegetable oil

1 cup (115 g) shredded mozzarella cheese

—

Serves 4

Lay the eggplant slices on a clean kitchen towel. Generously salt both sides of each slice and let sit for 30 minutes. Rinse the slices under cold water to remove the excess salt.

Spray a 7 × 3-inch (18 × 7.5 cm) baking dish with nonstick cooking spray. In a large bowl, stir together the ricotta, Parmesan, egg, parsley, garlic powder, salt, and pepper. Spread about ½ cup (120 ml) marinara sauce in the bottom of the prepared pan.

Preheat an outdoor grill, or grill pan, to medium heat. Lightly coat the eggplant slices with the vegetable oil. Grill for about 3 minutes per side until lightly browned and tender then transfer them to a work surface. Place a large dollop of cheese filling on the large end of each slice and wrap the eggplant around it. Place the eggplant rolls in the prepared pan, seam-side down. Top with the remaining ½ cup (120 ml) sauce and the mozzarella. Cover the pan with aluminum foil.

Place a trivet in the pressure cooking pot and add 1 cup (235 ml) water. Use a sling to place the dish on the trivet. Lock the lid in place. Select High Pressure and 8 minutes cook time.

When the cook time ends, turn off the pressure cooker. Let the pressure release naturally for 10 minutes and finish with a quick pressure release. When the valve drops, carefully remove the lid. Remove the dish from the cooking pot and serve.

TIP

Salting the eggplant before cooking draws out excess moisture so that your sauce and filling aren't too watery.

Brown Rice Fiesta Bake

A hearty meatless meal made with good-for-you brown rice and black beans. The tomatoes and green chilies give it a mildly spicy flavor, and the cheese finishes it with a gooey deliciousness.

1 tablespoon (15 ml) vegetable oil

1 large onion, diced

4 cloves garlic, minced or pressed

2 cans (10 ounces, or 284 g, each) mild diced tomatoes and green chilies

1 cup (235 ml) water

1 cup (190 g) brown rice

1 teaspoon chili powder

½ teaspoon ground cumin

½ teaspoon salt

¼ teaspoon freshly ground black pepper

1 cup (165 g) frozen corn, thawed

1 can (15 ounces, or 425 g) black beans, drained and rinsed

¼ cup (4 g) chopped fresh cilantro leaves

1½ cups (173 g) shredded Cheddar cheese

Sour cream and tortilla chips, for serving

—

Serves 6

Select Browning/Sauté and add the vegetable oil to the pressure cooking pot. When the oil is hot, add the onion. Sauté for about 3 minutes until the onion softens. Add the garlic and cook for 1 minute more. Stir in the tomatoes and green chilies, water, rice, chili powder, cumin, salt, and pepper. Lock the lid in place. Select High Pressure and 22 minutes cook time.

When the cook time ends, turn off the pressure cooker. Let the pressure release naturally for 10 minutes and finish with a quick pressure release. When the valve drops, carefully remove the lid.

Select Simmer/Sauté and stir in the corn and black beans. Cook for about 3 minutes until heated. Stir in the cilantro.

Preheat the broiler. Spray a 9 × 9-inch (23 × 23 cm) ovenproof dish with nonstick cooking spray. Pour the rice mixture into the prepared dish and top with the Cheddar. Broil until the cheese melts and starts to brown. Serve topped with sour cream and tortilla chips, if desired.

TIP

I like to use leftovers as a burrito filling for lunch the next day.

Three-Cheese Lasagna

Lasagna doesn't have to be time-consuming. No-boil noodles have this easy pressure cooker dish ready in half the time.

8 ounces (227 g) country-style sausage

1 can (14.5 ounces, or 411 g) diced tomatoes, well drained

1 can (8 fluid ounces, or 235 ml) tomato sauce

1 teaspoon garlic powder

1 teaspoon dried basil

¼ teaspoon red pepper flakes

¼ teaspoon salt

1 cup (250 g) part-skim ricotta cheese

1½ cups (173 g) shredded mozzarella cheese, divided

½ cup (40 g) shredded Parmesan cheese

1 large egg

6 no-boil lasagna noodles

—

Serves 4

Select Browning/Sauté and when hot, add the sausage. Cook for 5 minutes, stirring often to break up the meat, until the sausage is no longer pink. Drain excess fat from the pot. Stir in the tomatoes, tomato sauce, garlic powder, basil, red pepper flakes, and salt. Transfer to a large bowl and set aside. Wipe out the pressure cooking pot.

In another large bowl, mix together the ricotta cheese, ½ cup (57.5 g) mozzarella, the Parmesan, and egg until blended.

Spray a 7 × 3-inch (18 × 7.5 cm) round cake pan or 1½-quart (1.4 L) baking dish with nonstick cooking spray. Spread a thin layer of meat sauce on the bottom of the prepared pan. Break the noodles into pieces to form a single layer on top of the meat sauce. Spread another thin layer of sauce on the noodles. Spread half the cheese mixture on top of the sauce. Add a second layer of noodles, another thin layer of meat sauce, and the remaining cheese mixture. Top with a third layer of noodles and the remaining meat sauce, and finish with the remaining 1 cup (115 g) mozzarella. Cover the pan with aluminum foil.

Add 1 cup (235 ml) water to the pressure cooking pot and place a trivet in the bottom. Place the pan of lasagna on the trivet. Lock the lid in place. Select High Pressure and 20 minutes cook time.

When the cook time ends, turn off the pressure cooker. Let the pressure release naturally for 10 minutes and finish with a quick pressure release. When the valve drops, carefully remove the lid. Remove the lasagna pan from the cooking pot and let rest for 5 minutes before serving.

Fish en Papillote

Fish "en papillote" sounds fancy, but it's just fish cooked in parchment paper. Cooking it this way lets the fish cook deliciously in its own juices and butter!

4 (6 ounces, or 170 g, each) cod fillets, about 1 inch (2.5 cm) thick

Salt and freshly ground black pepper, for seasoning

¼ red onion, thinly sliced

1 lemon, thinly sliced, seeds removed

¼ cup (56 g) unsalted butter

4 sprigs fresh thyme or fresh dill

—

Serves 4

Place one fillet in the center of a 12 × 16-inch (30 × 40.5 cm) piece of parchment paper. Season with salt and pepper. Place about one-fourth of the red onion and lemon slices on the fillet. Top with 1 tablespoon (14 g) butter and 1 thyme sprig. Repeat with the remaining fillets.

Fold the parchment paper by bringing the opposite sides of the paper together in the center above the fish. Fold the top of the paper over and continue folding tightly until the paper reaches the fish, crimping to seal. Then roll and crimp the ends closed. Repeat to seal all packets.

Add 1 cup (235 ml) water to the pressure cooking pot and place a trivet in the bottom. Stack the 4 packets of fish on the trivet, with 2 on the rack and 2 stacked crosswise on top of those. Lock the lid in place. Select High Pressure and 8 minutes cook time.

When the cook time ends, turn off the pressure cooker. Let the pressure release naturally for 5 minutes and finish with a quick pressure release. When the valve drops, carefully remove the lid. Carefully remove and open the packets and serve immediately.

TIP

Flounder, tilapia, and haddock are other types of white fish that work well in this recipe. The fish won't brown like it would in the oven—instead, it retains its pretty pale-white color and stays tender and flaky.

CHAPTER 7

Desserts

*You don't always think of desserts when you think of pressure cooking, but the moist environment of the pressure cooker is perfect for cooking desserts such as rich, creamy cheesecakes, crème brûlée, and one of the most popular recipes on my blog, **Pressure Cooking Today**—old-fashioned rice pudding.*

Key Lime Pie

A classic pie with sour cream and lime zest added to give it just a little more zing.

For Crust:

¾ cup (45 g) graham cracker crumbs, about 6 crackers

3 tablespoons (42 g) unsalted butter, melted

1 tablespoon (12 g) sugar

For filling:

4 large egg yolks

1 can (14 fluid ounces, or 414 ml) sweetened condensed milk

½ cup (120 ml) fresh key lime juice

⅓ cup (75 g) sour cream

2 tablespoons (12 g) grated key lime zest

Whipped cream, for serving

—

Serves 6 to 8

Spray a 7-inch (18 cm) springform pan with nonstick cooking spray. Pour 1 cup (235 ml) water into the pressure cooking pot and place the trivet in the bottom.

TO MAKE THE CRUST: In a small bowl, stir together the graham cracker crumbs, butter, and sugar. Press the crust evenly in the bottom and slightly up the sides of the pan. Freeze for 10 minutes.

TO MAKE THE FILLING: In a large bowl, with a handheld mixer, beat the egg yolks until they are light yellow. Gradually beat in the sweetened condensed milk until thickened. Slowly add the lime juice and beat until smooth. Stir in the sour cream and lime zest. Pour the batter into the springform pan. Cover the pan with aluminum foil. Carefully center the filled pan on a sling and lower it into the pressure cooking pot. Fold the sling down so that it doesn't interfere with closing the lid. Lock the lid in place. Select High Pressure and 15 minutes cook time.

When the cook time ends, turn off the pressure cooker. Let the pressure release naturally for 10 minutes and finish with a quick pressure release. When the valve drops, carefully remove the lid. Transfer the springform pan to a wire rack to cool and remove the aluminum foil. When cooled, cover with plastic wrap and refrigerate for at least 4 hours or overnight. Serve topped with whipped cream.

TIP

If you can't find key limes, substitute ¼ cup (60 ml) fresh lemon juice and ¼ cup fresh lime juice.

Just Right Pumpkin Pie

A classic pumpkin pie filling in a crumbly Pecan Sandies cookie crust. When a big pumpkin pie is too much, this 7-inch (18 cm) pie is just right.

For Crust:

½ cup (93 g) crushed Pecan Sandies cookies (about 6 cookies)

⅓ cup (33 g) toasted pecans, chopped

2 tablespoons (28 g) unsalted butter, melted

For filling:

½ cup (120 g) packed light brown sugar

½ teaspoon salt

1½ teaspoons pumpkin pie spice

1 egg, beaten

1½ cups (368 g) pumpkin purée (also called solid pack pumpkin)

½ cup (120 ml) evaporated milk

Whipped cream, for serving

—

Serves 6 to 8

Spray a 7-inch (18 cm) springform pan with nonstick cooking spray. Pour 1 cup (235 ml) water into the pressure cooking pot and place the trivet in the bottom.

TO MAKE THE CRUST: In a small bowl, stir together the cookie crumbs, pecans, and butter. Spread the crust evenly in the bottom and about 1 inch (2.5 cm) up the sides of the pan. Freeze for 10 minutes.

TO MAKE THE FILLING: In a large bowl, combine the brown sugar, salt, and pumpkin pie spice. Whisk in the egg, pumpkin, and evaporated milk. Pour the batter into the springform pan. Cover the top with aluminum foil. Carefully center the filled pan on a sling and lower it into the cooking pot. Fold the sling down so that it doesn't interfere with closing the lid. Lock the lid in place. Select High Pressure and 35 minutes cook time.

When the cook time ends, turn off the pressure cooker. Let the pressure release naturally for 10 minutes and finish with a quick pressure release. When the valve drops, carefully remove the lid. Remove the pie and check that the middle is set. If not, return it to the cooker, relock the lid, and cook on High Pressure for 5 minutes more. Transfer the pie to a wire rack to cool and remove the foil. When cooled, cover with plastic wrap and refrigerate for at least 4 hours or overnight. Serve with whipped cream.

> **TIP**
>
> Change up the crust by using gingersnaps instead—really, most crisp, crumbly cookies work well.

Mini Creamy Lemon Pies

These pies are made creamy—and a little tangy—with yogurt, which contrasts nicely with the crumbly graham cracker crust. If you love key lime pie, you'll go crazy for this lemon version.

For Crust:

1 cup (60 g) graham cracker crumbs, about 8 crackers

1 tablespoon (12 g) sugar

¼ cup (55 g) unsalted butter, melted

For Filling:

4 large egg yolks

1 can (14 fluid ounces, or 414 ml) sweetened condensed milk

½ cup (120 ml) fresh lemon juice

¼ cup (60 g) plain Greek yogurt

2 tablespoons (12 g) grated lemon zest

Whipped cream, for serving

—

Serves 6 to 8

Pour 1 cup (235 ml) water into the pressure cooking pot and place the trivet in the pot.

TO MAKE THE CRUST: In a medium-size bowl, mix together the graham cracker crumbs, butter, and sugar until well blended. Divide the crust evenly among 6 (6-ounce, or 170 g) custard cups. Press the crust evenly in the bottom and slightly up the sides. Freeze for 10 minutes.

TO MAKE THE FILLING: In a large bowl, beat the egg yolks until they are pale yellow. Gradually beat in the sweetened condensed milk. Add the lemon juice and beat until smooth. Whisk in the yogurt and lemon zest. Divide among the custard cups. Place 3 cups on the trivet and put a second trivet on top. Place the remaining 3 cups on it. Lock the lid in place. Select High Pressure and 4 minutes cook time.

When the cook time ends, turn off the pressure cooker. Let the pressure release naturally for 10 minutes and finish with a quick pressure release. When the valve drops, carefully remove the lid. Transfer the cups to a wire rack to cool. Use a paper towel to soak up any water that may have accumulated on the tops of the pies. When cool, cover the pies with plastic wrap and refrigerate for at least 2 hours. Serve topped with whipped cream.

> **TIP**
>
> You could substitute sour cream for the Greek yogurt in this recipe.

Peanut Butter Cup Cheesecake

This cheesecake is smooth, rich, and creamy—a little slice is all you need to satisfy your peanut butter cup craving.

For Crust:

1 cup Oreo cookie crumbs (about 12 cookies, 5 ounces, or 142 g)

2 tablespoons (28 g) unsalted butter, melted

For Filling:

12 ounces (340 g) cream cheese, at room temperature

½ cup (100 g) sugar

½ cup (130 g) smooth peanut butter

¼ cup (60 ml) heavy cream

1½ teaspoons vanilla extract

1 tablespoon (7 g) all-purpose flour

2 large eggs, at room temperature

1 egg yolk, at room temperature

For Ganache:

6 ounces (170 g) milk chocolate, finely chopped, divided

⅓ cup (78 ml) heavy cream

⅔ cup (about 3½ ounces, or 99 g) coarsely chopped peanut butter cups

—
Serves 8

Spray a 7-inch (18 cm) springform pan with nonstick cooking spray. Pour 1 cup (235 ml) water into the pressure cooking pot and place a trivet in the bottom.

TO MAKE THE CRUST: In a small bowl, stir together the cookie crumbs and butter. Spread the crust evenly in the bottom and about 1 inch (2.5 cm) up the side of the prepared pan. Freeze for 10 minutes.

TO MAKE THE FILLING: In a large bowl, with a handheld mixer, mix the cream cheese and sugar at medium speed until smooth. Blend in the peanut butter, heavy cream, vanilla, and flour. One at a time, mix in the eggs and egg yolk, mixing until just blended—do not overmix. Pour the batter over the crust. Cover the pan with aluminum foil. Carefully center the filled pan on a sling and lower it into the cooking pot. Fold the sling down so that it doesn't interfere with closing the lid. Lock the lid in place. Select High Pressure and 50 minutes cook time.

When the cook time ends, turn off the pressure cooker. Let the pressure release naturally for 10 minutes and finish with a quick pressure release. When the valve drops, carefully remove the lid.

Use an instant-read thermometer to check that the cheesecake has reached 150°F (65.5°C) in the center. If not, relock the lid and cook the cheesecake at High Pressure for 5 minutes more, using a second 10-minute natural pressure release. Transfer

> **TIP**
>
> I use mini peanut butter cups and cut them in half, rather than unwrapping and chopping the bigger peanut butter cups. Use whichever you'd prefer.

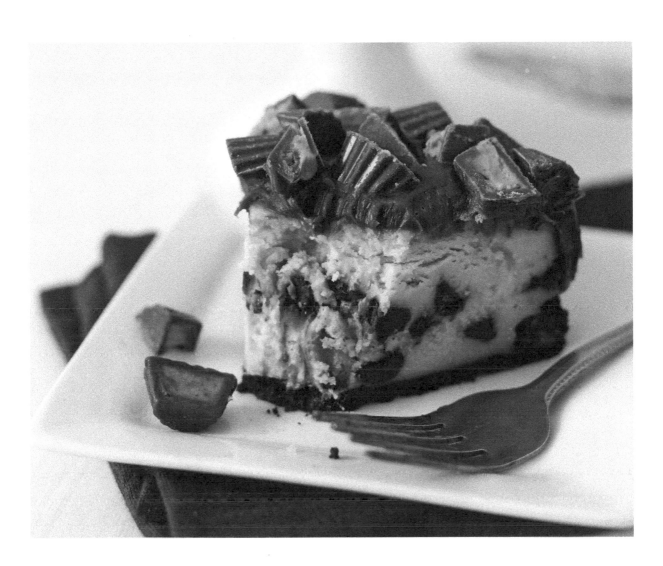

the cheesecake to a wire rack to cool. Remove the aluminum foil. When cooled, cover with plastic wrap and refrigerate for at least 4 hours or overnight.

TO MAKE THE GANACHE: Place 3 ounces (85 g) of the chocolate in a large bowl. In a small saucepan over medium-high heat, bring the heavy cream to a boil. Immediately remove it from the heat and pour it over the chocolate. Stir until the chocolate melts completely. Add the remaining 3 ounces (85 g) chocolate and stir until it melts completely. Cool until the ganache thickens but is still thin enough to drip down the sides of the cheesecake. Spoon the ganache over the cheesecake, spreading it to the edges and letting it drip down the sides. Pile the chopped peanut butter cups on top. Refrigerate until ready to serve.

Cranberry-Orange Bread Pudding

A decadent bread pudding made with bread and croissants, flavored with orange zest and dried cranberries, and served with a heavenly crème anglaise.

For Pudding:

Butter, for greasing the dish

3 large eggs

½ cup (100 g) sugar

1 teaspoon vanilla extract

Zest of 1 orange

2 cups (470 ml) heavy cream

3 large croissants, torn into bite-size pieces

6 slices white bread, cubed

¼ cup (30 g) dried cranberries

For Crème Anglaise:

¾ cup (175 ml) heavy cream

¼ cup (60 ml) milk

2 egg yolks

⅓ cup (67 g) sugar

1 teaspoon vanilla bean paste or extract

—
Serves 8

Generously grease a 1½-quart (1.4 L) glass or metal baking dish with butter. (Be sure the dish fits in your pressure cooking pot.)

TO MAKE THE PUDDING: In a large bowl, whisk the eggs, sugar, vanilla, and orange zest. Whisk in the heavy cream. Gently stir in the croissants, bread, and cranberries. Pour into the prepared dish.

Pour 1 cup (235 ml) water into the pressure cooking pot and place a trivet in the bottom. Center the dish on a sling and carefully lower it into the cooking pot. Lock the lid in place. Select High Pressure and 30 minutes cook time.

When the cook time ends, turn off the pressure cooker. Let the pressure release naturally for 10 minutes and finish with a quick pressure release. When the valve drops, carefully remove the lid. Remove the dish from the cooking pot and let cool for at least 15 minutes more before serving.

TO MAKE THE CRÈME ANGLAISE: In a small saucepan over medium heat, whisk the heavy cream and milk. Cook until the mixture just starts to boil. Remove from the heat.

In a medium-size bowl, whisk the egg yolks and sugar. Whisk in half the hot milk mixture. Add the egg mixture to the saucepan and cook over medium heat, stirring constantly, until the sauce comes to a boil. Reduce the heat to low and simmer for about 2 minutes until the sauce thickens slightly. Remove from the heat and stir in the vanilla. Set aside.

Slice the bread pudding into wedges and drizzle each slice with crème anglaise.

Cinnamon–Zucchini Bread with Cinnamon Icing

In late summer, when your garden overflows with zucchini, the last thing you want to do is turn on the oven and heat up the house. Instead, "bake" your zucchini bread in the pressure cooker.

2 cups (224 g) all-purpose flour

2 teaspoons ground cinnamon

1½ teaspoons baking powder

½ teaspoon salt

½ cup (100 g) sugar

½ cup (120 g) packed light brown sugar

⅔ cup (157 ml) vegetable oil

2 large eggs

1 teaspoon vanilla extract

½ cup (115 g) sour cream

1 cup (120 g) grated zucchini

½ cup (50 g) pecans, chopped and toasted, plus more for serving

¾ cup (90 g) powdered sugar

Pinch ground cinnamon

1 tablespoon (15 ml) milk

—
Serves 8

Spray a half-size (1.4 L) Bundt pan with nonstick cooking spray. In a small bowl, whisk the flour, cinnamon, baking powder, and salt. Set aside.

In a large bowl, whisk the sugar, brown sugar, vegetable oil, eggs, and vanilla until blended. Whisk in the sour cream. Add the dry ingredients and whisk until just blended. Stir in the zucchini and pecans. Spoon the batter evenly into the prepared pan. Cover the pan with a paper towel and cover both the paper towel and the pan with aluminum foil crimped tightly around the edges.

Pour 1 cup (235 ml) water into the pressure cooker and place a trivet in the bottom. Use a sling to carefully lower the Bundt pan onto the trivet. Lock the lid in place. Select High Pressure and 35 minutes cook time.

When the cook time ends, turn off the pressure cooker. Let the pressure release naturally for 10 minutes and finish with a quick pressure release. When the valve drops, carefully remove the lid. Check the bread for doneness. An instant-read thermometer inserted into the middle should be about 210°F (99°C) or a toothpick inserted into the center should come out clean. If the bread is not done, replace the foil, relock the lid, and cook on High Pressure for 5 more minutes. Carefully transfer the Bundt pan to a wire rack to cool, uncovered, for 10 minutes. Remove the bread from the pan and cool completely on a wire rack.

Right before serving, in a small bowl, whisk the powdered sugar, cinnamon, and milk until smooth. Pour the icing over the bread. Decorate with chopped pecans, if desired.

TIP

Removing excess moisture from the zucchini is essential for a good zucchini bread. I like to use a salad spinner or wrap the grated zucchini in a clean kitchen towel to squeeze out excess water.

Fudgy Brownies

Rich, dense, and fudgy brownies to satisfy your chocolate craving. It's easy to make in one bowl.

6 tablespoons (85 g) unsalted butter

1 cup (200 g) sugar

⅓ cup (29 g) unsweetened cocoa powder

2 tablespoons (30 ml) water

1 teaspoon vanilla extract

2 large eggs

1 cup (112 g) all-purpose flour

½ teaspoon baking powder

¼ teaspoon salt

½ cup (87 g) semisweet chocolate chips

Ice cream and powdered sugar, for serving

—

Serves 8

Spray a 7 × 3-inch (18 × 7.5 cm) round cake pan with nonstick cooking spray. Line the bottom with parchment paper.

In a large microwave-safe bowl, microwave the butter for about 1 minute until melted. Stir in the sugar and microwave for 1 minute more. Whisk in the cocoa powder, water, and vanilla until smooth. Whisk in the eggs. Add the flour, baking powder, and salt. Stir until just smooth. Mix in the chocolate chips.

Spread the batter into the prepared pan. Pour 1 cup (235 ml) water into the pressure cooker and place a trivet in the bottom. Use a sling to carefully lower the pan onto the trivet. Lock the lid in place. Select High Pressure and 20 minutes cook time.

When the cook time ends, turn off the pressure cooker. Let the pressure release naturally for 10 minutes and finish with a quick pressure release. When the valve drops, carefully remove the lid.

Transfer the pan to a wire rack to cool for 10 minutes. Invert the brownies onto a serving plate and carefully peel off the parchment paper. Cool to room temperature and serve topped with ice cream or a sprinkle of powdered sugar, if desired.

TIP

Parchment paper is coated with silicone, so it is nonstick. It isn't essential for this recipe, but it does make cleanup a lot easier. You can buy it in rolls at the grocery store, but I prefer precut flat sheets.

About the Author

Barbara Schieving lives in a suburb of Salt Lake City, Utah, with her husband of 39 years, who is often in the kitchen with her. He likes to refer to himself as her slicer and dicer. They have four grown children and two adorable grandsons.

She is the creator of two popular recipe blogs: her pressure cooking site, PressureCookingToday.com, where she shares fabulous, family-friendly recipes for the electric pressure cooker/Instant Pot; and BarbaraBakes.com, where she shares her passion for baking. *Pressure Cooking Today* and *Barbara Bakes* receive over 1.5 million pageviews each month. Over the past eight years, her distinctive recipes and conversational style have earned her a dedicated readership across the globe.

Index

CPSIA information can be obtained
at www.ICGtesting.com
Printed in the USA
LVHW011108130123
736628LV00004B/4